Quilting the
Lodge Look

LANDAUER BOOKS

Quilting the Lodge Look

by Debbie Field
for Granola Girl® Designs

This book was designed, produced, and published by Landauer Books
A division of Landauer Corporation
12251 Maffitt Road, Cumming, Iowa 50061

President/Publisher: Jeramy Lanigan Landauer
Director of Operations: Kitty Jacobson
Editor-in-Chief: Becky Johnston
Creative Director: Laurel Albright
Technical Illustrator: Linda L. Bender
Copy Editor: Connie McCall
Photographers: Craig Anderson and Dennis Kennedy
Photostylists: DeWayne Studer and Laurel Albright

ISBN: 1-890621-74-9
This book is printed on acid-free paper.
Printed in China

10 9 8 7 6 5 4 3 2 1

Library of Congress Control Number: 2004111334

INTRODUCTION

Let your love of nature be the inspiration for lodge-look decorating themes throughout your home and garden.

On the following pages you'll find nine 21" x 21" patchwork quilt blocks inspired by traditional nature-themed block patterns such as Bear Paw, Flying Geese, Maple Leaf and Log Cabin—each with its own appliquéd scene celebrating wildlife and the great outdoors. You can assemble all nine blocks into a fabulous sampler quilt, MEMORIES FROM THE LODGE or choose four favorite blocks to make a wallhanging. The sampler quilt sets the scene for smaller projects using one or more of the wonderful wildlife appliqué scenes such as Portaging, Lonely Loon, Fall's First Frost, Hike for a Better View, and Catch of the Day.

For an added bonus, I've created a collection of snuggler quilts—just the right size for comfortable evenings in front of the fire or watching a favorite movie.

Whether you start small by choosing a favorite small project or capture the essence of several blocks to create one spectacular wildlife habitat quilt or wallhanging, I'm sure that you'll enjoy quilting the lodge look as much as I do!

Debbie Field

Contents

MEMORIES FROM THE LODGE

BLOCKS & PROJECTS

The traditional Crossed Canoes block takes you on a portaging adventure with patterns for everything from campsite to canoes to appliqué on a 4-block snuggler, pillow and placemats.

An all-time favorite, the Flying Geese Block is featured in a 9-block snuggler and the background for an outback cabin and aspen trees to appliqué on a wilderness wallhanging.

Make the Bear Paw Block your catch of the day featured as a 24-block snuggler and appliqué patterns for a bear bath set complete with bear tracks stenciled on a cotton rug.

The Log Cabin block set on point is an easy way to build a stunning 6-block snuggler and the perfect background to appliqué a lonely loon and lilies on a waterfowl wallhanging and bath set.

Memories From the Lodge
Quilt

Memories from the Lodge Quilt

Materials

Finished size is approximately 84" x 84"

Fabrics are based on 42"-wide cotton fabric that has not been washed.

9 completed blocks

■

1/4 yard of brown fabric for the cornerstones

■

1 yard of tan fabric for sashing

■

2-3/4 yards of print for
the outer border and the binding

■

Queen size batting

■

8 yards of fabric for backing (seamed to fit)

Cutting Instructions

(A 1/4" seam allowance is included in these measurements.)

• From the brown fabric, cut:
  1 strip 2-1/2" x 42"; from this strip, cut:
  16 squares 2-1/2" x 2-1/2"

• From the tan fabric, cut:
  12 strips 2-1/2" x 42"; from these strips, cut:
  24 rectangles 2-1/2" x 21-1/2" for sashing

• From the print fabric, cut:
  9 strips 6-1/2" x 42" for the outer border
  9 strips 3" x 42" for the binding

Assembling the Quilt top

1. Sew groups of three blocks and four sashing strips together, as shown. Press toward the sashing strips. You will have three rows total.

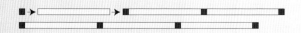

2. Sew four cornerstones and three sashing strips together, as shown. Press toward the sashing strips. You will have four completed sashing strips.

3. Sew the rows and sashing strips together, as shown. Press toward the sashing strips.

Adding the Borders

1. Measure the width of the quilt top through the center to get top and bottom border measurement. Cut two strips to that measurement from the 6-1/2" print

border strips. Sew border strips to the top and bottom. Press toward the border.

2. Measure the length of the quilt top through the center to get side border measurement. Cut two strips to that measurement from the 6-1/2" print border strips. Sew the border strips to each side. Press toward the border.

Finishing the Quilt

1. Layer the quilt backing fabric, batting, and quilt top. Baste the layers together.

2. Hand- or machine-quilt as desired.

3. Finish the quilt by sewing on the binding.

Quilt it Quick

4-Block Wallhanging

Materials

Finished size is approximately 54" x 54"

Fabrics are based on 42"-wide cotton fabric that has not been washed.

4 completed blocks

■

1/8 yard of dark red fabric for the cornerstones

■

5/8 yard of cream fabric for sashing

■

1-1/2 yards of dark teal fabric for the outer border and the binding

■

60" x 60" piece of batting

■

3 1/2 yards of fabric for backing (seamed to fit)

Cutting Instructions

• From the dark red fabric, cut:
  1 strip 2-1/2" x 42"; from this strip, cut:
    9 squares 2-1/2" x 2-1/2" for cornerstones

• From the cream fabric, cut:
  7 strips 2-1/2" x 42"; from these strips, cut:
    12 rectangles 2-1/2" x 21-1/2" for sashing

• From the dark teal fabric, cut:
  6 strips 4-1/2" x 42" for border
  6 strips 2-3/4" x 42" for binding

Assembling the Wallhanging

1. Sew groups of two blocks and three sashing strips together, as shown. Press toward the sashing strips. You will have two rows total.

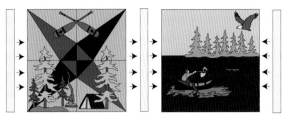

2. Sew three cornerstones and two sashing strips together, as shown. Press toward the sashing strips. You will have three completed sashing strips.

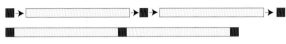

3. Sew the rows and sashing strips together, as shown. Press toward the sashing strips.

Adding the Borders

1. Measure the width of the quilt top through the center to get top and bottom border measurement. Cut two strips to that measurement from the 4-1/2" print border strips. Sew border strips to the top and bottom. Press toward the border.

2. Measure the length of the quilt top through the center to get side border measurement. Cut two strips to that measurement. Press toward the outside.

Finishing the Wallhanging

1. Layer quilt backing fabric, batting, and top.

2. Quilt and bind.

CROSSED CANOES

The traditional Crossed Canoes block takes you on a portaging adventure with patterns for everything from campsite to canoes to appliqué on a 4-block snuggler, pillow and placemats.

Materials

Finished size is approximately 21" x 21"

Fabrics are based on 42"-wide cotton fabric that has not been washed.

3/4 yard of light tan fabric for background

■

1/4 yard of dark red fabric for canoes

■

1/4 yard of dark green fabric for canoes

■

1/4 yard total of 2 shades of green fabric for trees

■

Scraps of light and dark blue fabric for tent, water

■

Scraps of brown fabric for logs in campfire

■

Scrap of gray fabric for smoke

■

Scrap of red fabric for flame

■

Scrap of gold fabric for canoe paddles

■

Scraps of red, black, and blue fabric for trim on paddles

■

1 yard of fusible web

■

Stabilizer for appliqués

■

Sulky® threads to match appliqué fabrics

Crossed Canoes Block

Cutting Instructions

(A 1/4" seam allowance is included in these measurements.)

• From the light tan fabric, cut:
  2 strips 11" x 42"; from these strips, cut:
  4 squares 11" x 11"

• From the dark red fabric, cut:
  1 strip 3-1/2" x 42"; from this strip, cut:
  2 squares 3-1/2" x 3-1/2"

• From the dark green fabric, cut:
  1 strip 3-1/2" x 42"; from this strip, cut:
  2 squares 3-1/2" x 3-1/2"

Assembling the Block

1. Diagonally mark the wrong side of the red and green 3-1/2" squares.

2. Place a red 3-1/2" square on a corner of an 11" light tan square. Sew on the diagonal line. Press the red square toward the outside. Trim away the middle triangle only. You will have 2 Unit A's.

Unit A

3. Repeat step 2, using the green 3-1/2" squares. You will have 2 Unit B's.

Unit B

Adding the Appliqués

1. Trace all appliqué templates from pages 18-21 and cut them out.

2. Refer to General Instructions to prepare pieces for appliqué.

3. Use lightweight tear-away stabilizer to machine-appliqué the pieces. Place the stabilizer beneath the fabric layers and use a small zigzag stitch to sew around each shape, smoothly covering the raw fabric edge. If your machine has stitch options, use them to detail the appliqués. After the stitching is complete, remove the stabilizer according to the manufacturer's instructions.

4. On the Unit A background squares, appliqué a green canoe point to the red triangle to make Unit A. You will have 2 Unit A's.

5. On the Unit B background squares, appliqué a dark red canoe point to the green triangle to make Unit B. You will have 2 Unit B's.

6. Sew a Unit A and a Unit B together. Press toward Unit A. You will have 2 Unit C's.

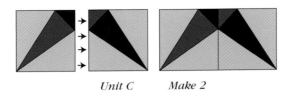

Unit C   *Make 2*

7. Sew two Unit C's together to make Unit D. Press in the direction of least amount of bulk.

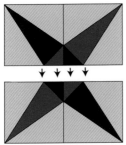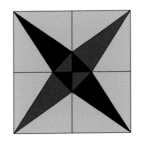

Unit D

8. Follow the illustration to position remaining appliqué pieces in place on the block. Stitch around the appliqué pieces with a small zigzag stitch to finish rough edges.

Templates for Crossed Canoes Block

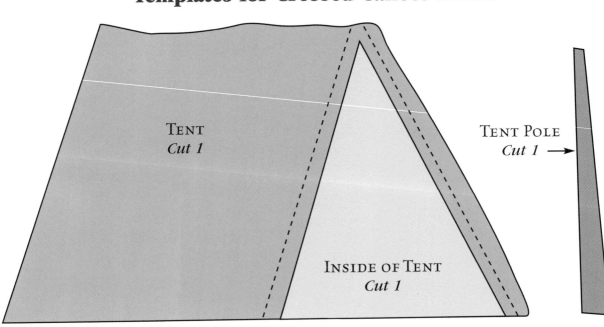

TENT
Cut 1

TENT POLE
Cut 1 →

INSIDE OF TENT
Cut 1

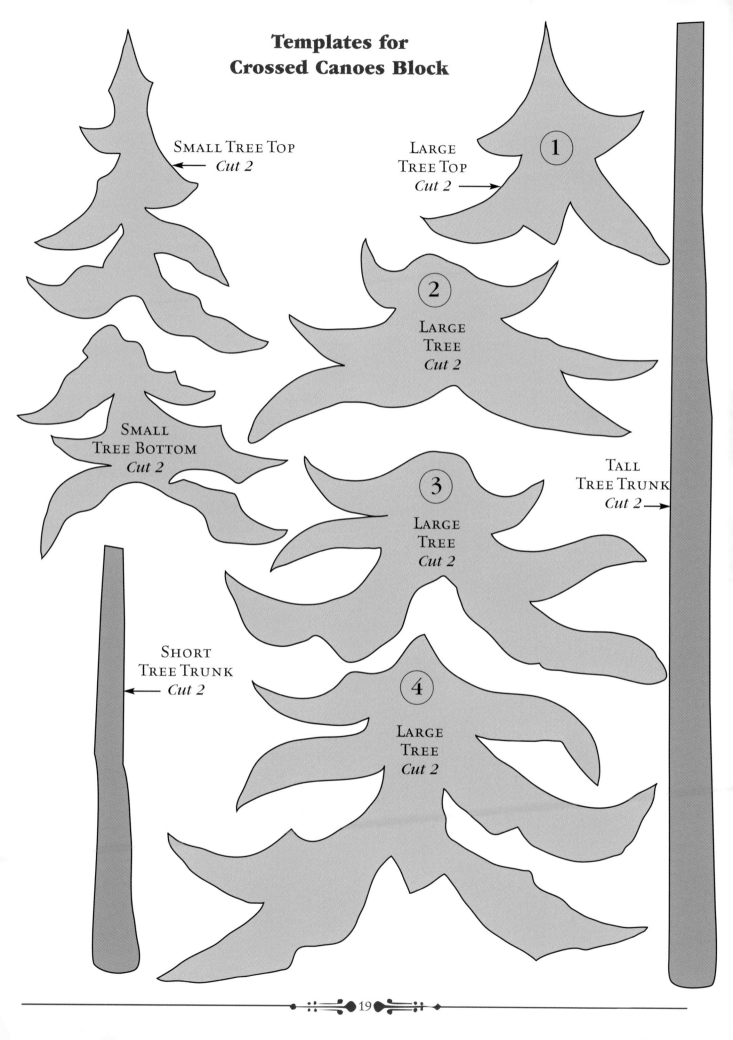

Templates for Crossed Canoes Block

SMALL TREE TOP
Cut 2

LARGE
TREE TOP
Cut 2

①

② LARGE
TREE
Cut 2

SMALL
TREE BOTTOM
Cut 2

③ LARGE
TREE
Cut 2

TALL
TREE TRUNK
Cut 2

SHORT
TREE TRUNK
Cut 2

④ LARGE
TREE
Cut 2

Templates for Crossed Canoes Block

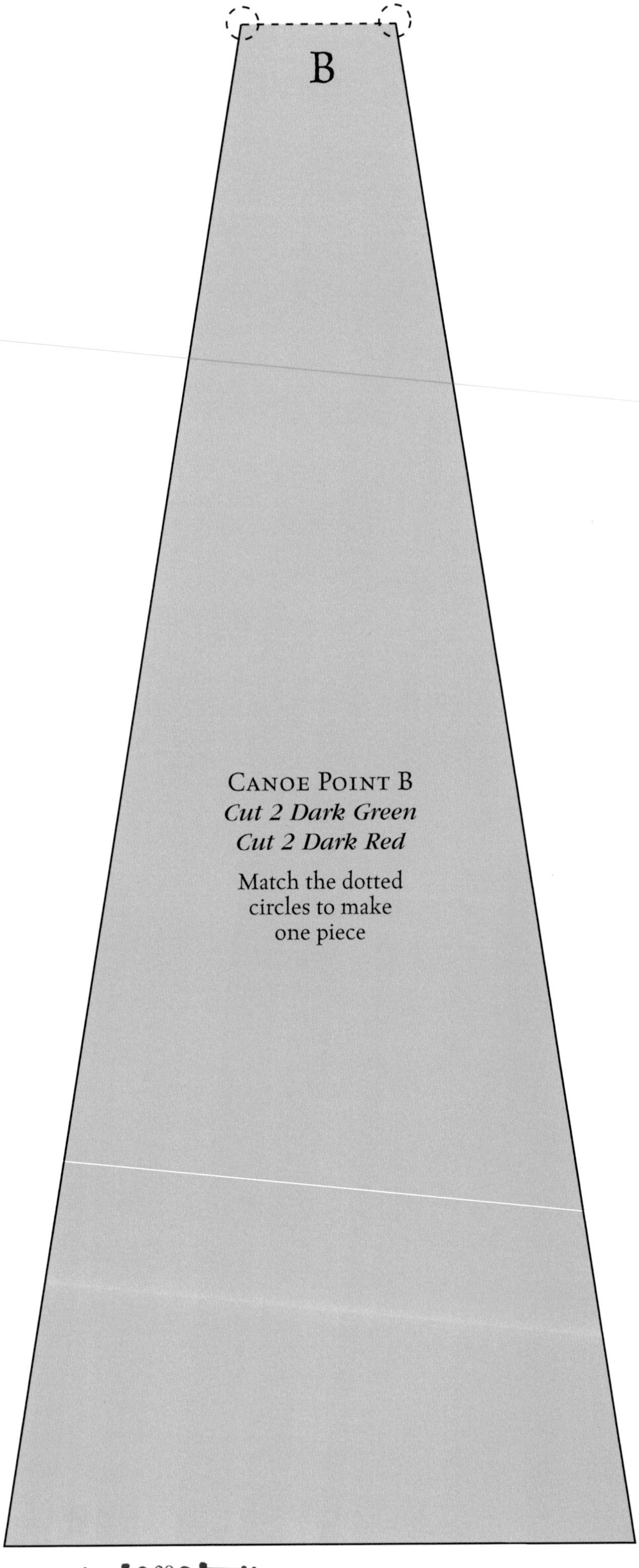

B

CANOE POINT A
Cut 2 Dark Green
Cut 2 Dark Red

Match the dotted
circles to make
one piece

A

CANOE POINT B
Cut 2 Dark Green
Cut 2 Dark Red

Match the dotted
circles to make
one piece

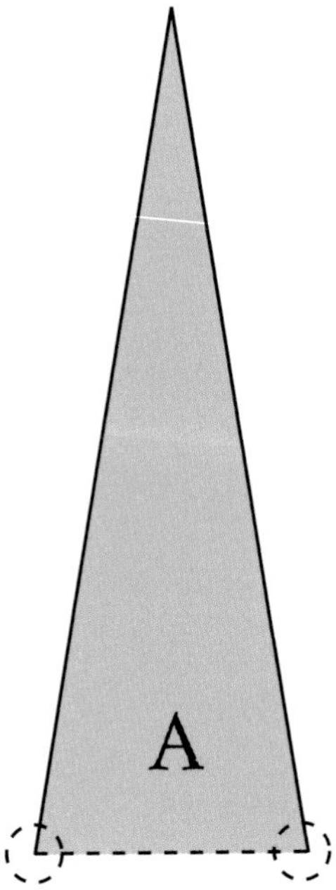

Templates for
Crossed Canoes Block

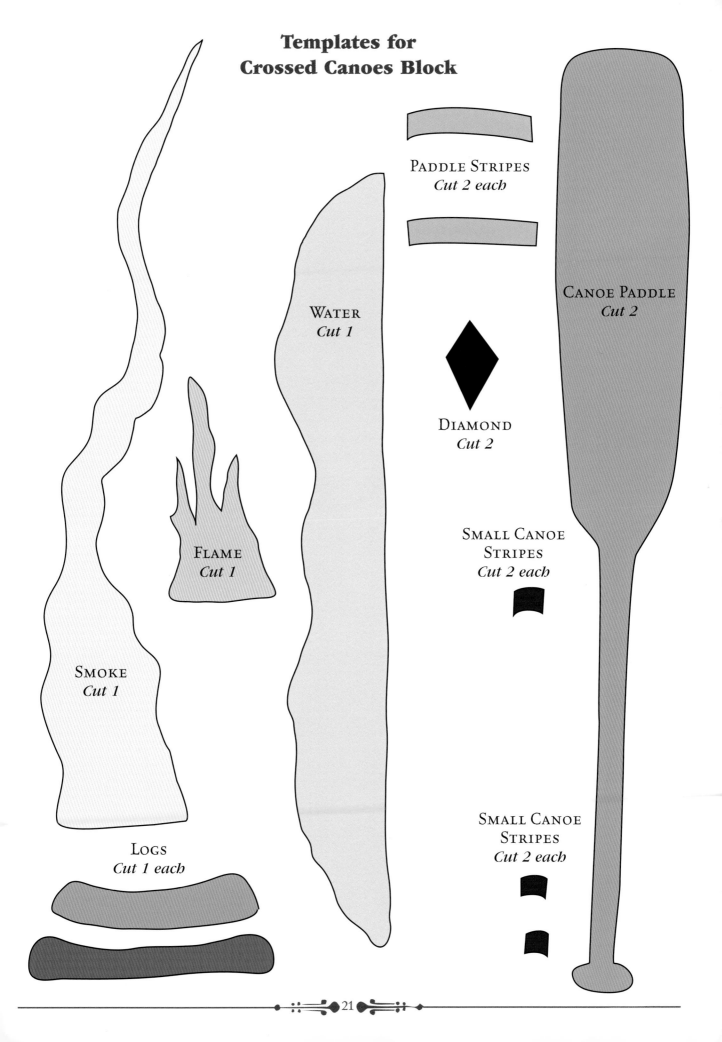

PADDLE STRIPES
Cut 2 each

WATER
Cut 1

DIAMOND
Cut 2

CANOE PADDLE
Cut 2

FLAME
Cut 1

SMALL CANOE
STRIPES
Cut 2 each

SMOKE
Cut 1

LOGS
Cut 1 each

SMALL CANOE
STRIPES
Cut 2 each

CANOE SNUGGLER

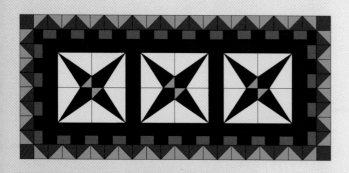

Materials

Finished size is approximately 72" x 72"

Fabrics are based on 40"-wide flannel fabric that has not been washed.

2 yards of tan flannel for background

■

3 yards of dark dark red flannel for canoe points, sashing, outside border and binding

■

1/2 yard of brown flannel for checkerboard border

■

1/2 yard of black flannel for checkerboard border

■

7/8 yard of gold flannel for canoe centers and triangle border

■

7/8 yard of green flannel for triangle border

■

1-3/4 yards of fusible web

■

82" x 82" piece of batting

■

5 yards of flannel for backing

■

Sulky® threads to match canoe appliqués

Canoe Block

Make 4

Cutting Instructions

(A 1/4" seam allowance is included in measurements.)

- From the tan flannel, cut:
    6 strips 10-1/2" x 40"; from these strips, cut:
        16 squares 10-1/2" x 10-1/2"

- From the dark red flannel, cut:
    1 strip 3-1/2" x 40"; from this strip, cut:
        8 squares 3-1/2" x 3-1/2"
    13 strips 4-1/2" x 40" for sashing and outside border
    8 strips 3" x 40" for binding

- From the brown flannel, cut:
    4 strips 2-1/2" x 40"; from these strips, cut:
        27 rectangles 2-1/2" x 4-1/2"

- From the black flannel, cut:
    4 strips 2-1/2" x 40"; from these strips, cut:
        27 rectangles 2-1/2" x 4-1/2"

- From the gold flannel, cut:
    1 strip 3-1/2" x 40"; from this strip, cut:
        8 squares 3-1/2" x 3-1/2"
    4 strips 4-7/8" x 40"; from these strips, cut:
        28 squares 4-7/8" x 4-7/8"; cut squares in half diagonally to make 56 half-square triangles.

- From the green flannel, cut:
    1 strip 4-1/2" x 40"; from this strip, cut:
        4 squares 4-1/2" x 4-1/2"
    4 strip 4-7/8" x 40"; from these strips, cut:
        28 squares 4-7/8" x 4-7/8"; cut squares in half diagonally to make 56 half-square triangles.

Assembling the Blocks

1. Draw a diagonal line on the back of the 8 gold squares 3-1/2" x 3-1/2" and the 8 dark red 3-1/2" x 3-1/2" squares.

2. Place a dark red 3-1/2" square on a corner of a 10-1/2" tan square. Sew on the diagonal line. Press the dark red square toward the outside. Trim away the middle triangle only. You will need 8 Unit A's.

Unit A   Make 8

3. Repeat step 2, using the gold 3-1/2" squares. You will need 8 Unit B's.

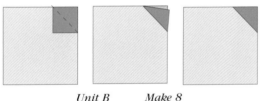

Unit B   Make 8

Appliquéing the Canoes to the Blocks

1. Trace canoe point appliqué from page 20 and cut out.

2. Trace 16 canoe points onto fusible web. Fuse to dark red flannel. Cut out the points and position them on the tan squares. See illustration for placement. Stitch around appliqués with a small zigzag stitch.

3. Sew a Unit A and a Unit B together, as shown. Press toward Unit A. You will need 8 Unit C's.

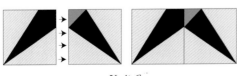

Unit C

4. Sew 2 Unit C's together. Press in the direction of least amount of bulk. You will need 4 Unit D's. The canoe blocks should measure 20-1/2" to each unfinished edge.

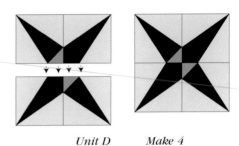

Unit D   Make 4

Adding the Sashing and Inner Borders

1. Cut 2 dark red 20-1/2" sashing rectangles from the dark red 4-1/2" x 40" strips.

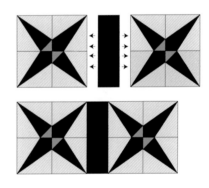

2. Sew the sashing rectangles between 2 Unit D's. Press toward the sashing. You will need 2 rows.

3. Seaming as needed, cut 3 dark red 44-1/2" sashing strips from the dark red 4-1/2" x 40" strips.

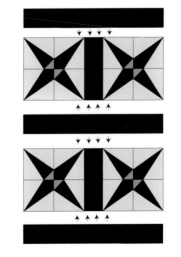

4. Sew the strips and rows together. Press toward the sashing strips.

5. Seaming the strips as needed, cut 2 dark red strips 52-1/2" from the dark red 4-1/2" x 40" strips. Sew to each side of quilt top and press toward the sashing.

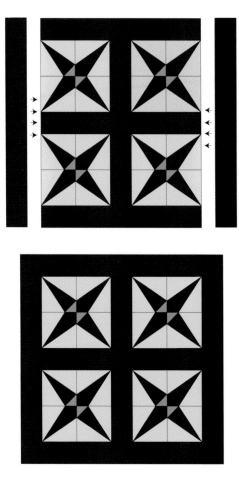

6. Using 13 brown 2-1/2" x 4-1/2" rectangles and 13 black 2-1/2" x 4-1/2" rectangles make 2 checked borders for the top and bottom. Press. For the bottom border use 6 brown and 7 black 2-1/2" x 4-1/2" rectangles. For the top border use 7 brown rectangles and 6 black 2-1/2" x 4-1/2" rectangles.

7. Sew the rows to the top and bottom of the quilt top. Press toward the border.

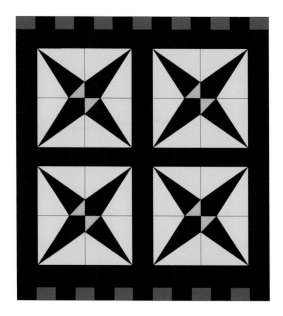

8. Using 14 brown 2-1/2" x 4-1/2" rectangles and 14 black 2-1/2" x 4-1/2" rectangles make two borders for the sides. Press. Use 7 brown rectangles and 7 black 2-1/2" x 4-1/2" rectangles for each side border.

9. For the triangle border, sew the gold 4-7/8" half-square triangles and the green 4-7/8" half-square triangles together. Press toward the green. You will need 56 Unit E's.

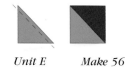

Unit E   Make 56

10. Sew 2 Unit E's together. Press in the direction of least amount of bulk. You will need 28 Unit F's for the triangle border.

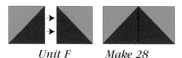

Unit F   Make 28

11. Sew 7 Unit F's together. Press in the direction of least amount of bulk. You will have 4 rows of Unit G.

Unit G   Make 28

12. Sew a green 4-1/2" square on each end of two of the Unit G's. Press toward the green. You will have 2 Unit H's.

Unit H   Make 2

13. Sew a Unit G on the top and bottom of the quilt top. Press toward the triangle border.

14. Sew a Unit H on each side of the quilt top. Press toward the triangle border.

Adding the Outer Borders

1. Measure the width of the the quilt top through the center to get the top and bottom outside border measurement. Cut 2 border strips to that length from the dark red 4-1/2" x 40" strips. Sew the border strips to the top and bottom of quilt. Press toward the border.

2. Measure the length of the quilt top through the center to get side border measurement. Cut 2 border strips that length from the dark red 4-1/2" x 40" strips. Sew to each side of the quilt. Press toward the border.

Finishing the Quilt

1. Layer the quilt backing fabric, the batting, and the quilt top. Baste the layers together.

2. Hand- or machine-quilt as desired.

3. Finish the quilt by sewing on the binding.

Canoe Snuggler

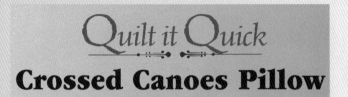

Quilt it Quick
Crossed Canoes Pillow

Materials

Finished size is approximately 17" x 17"

Fabrics are based on 42"-wide cotton fabric that has not been washed.

3/8 yard of cream fabric for pillow center

∎

1/8 yard of dark green fabric for inner border

∎

Scraps of dark red, green, brown, gold, blue, and black fabric for appliqués

∎

1 yard of dark red fabric for outer border and pillow back

∎

16" x 16" pillow form

∎

20" x 20" square of batting

∎

3/4 yard of fusible web

∎

Sulky® threads to match appliqué fabrics

Cutting Instructions

• From the cream fabric, cut:
  12" x 12" square

• From the dark green fabric, cut:
  2 strips 1-3/4" x 42" for inner border

• From the dark red fabric, cut:
  2 strips 2-1/4" x 42" for the outer border

Assembling the Pillow

1. Trace all appliqué templates from pages 28-29 and cut them out.

2. Refer to General Instructions to prepare pieces for appliqué.

3. Arrange appliqué pieces onto the cream 12" x 12" square. Stitch around appliqués with a small zigzag stitch.

4. For the inner border, measure the width of the pillow top through the center to get the top and bottom measurement. Cut 2 border strips to that length from the dark green 1-3/4" x 42" strips. Sew to the top and bottom of the pillow. Press toward the outside. Measure the length of the pillow through the center and cut 2 strips to that length from the dark green 1-3/4" x 44" strips. Sew to the sides of pillow.

5. For the outer border, measure the width of the pillow top through the center for the top and bottom measurement. Cut 2 border strips that length from the dark red 2-1/4" x 42" strips. Sew to the top and bottom of the pillow. Press toward the outside. Measure the length of the pillow through the center and cut 2 strips that length from the dark red 2-1/4" x 42" strips. Sew to the sides of the pillow.

Finishing the Pillow

1. Layer batting and pillow top. Quilt as desired.

2. Press and trim excess batting from pillow top. Layer backing (right side up) and pillow top wrong side up. Stitch 1/4" seam around pillow top, leaving bottom open to insert pillow form or fiberfill. Clip corners and trim away any excess backing fabric.

3. Turn to right side. Insert pillow form and stitch opening closed.

CANOE

RENTAL

Placement Diagram

CANOE
RENTAL

Templates for Canoe Rental Pillow

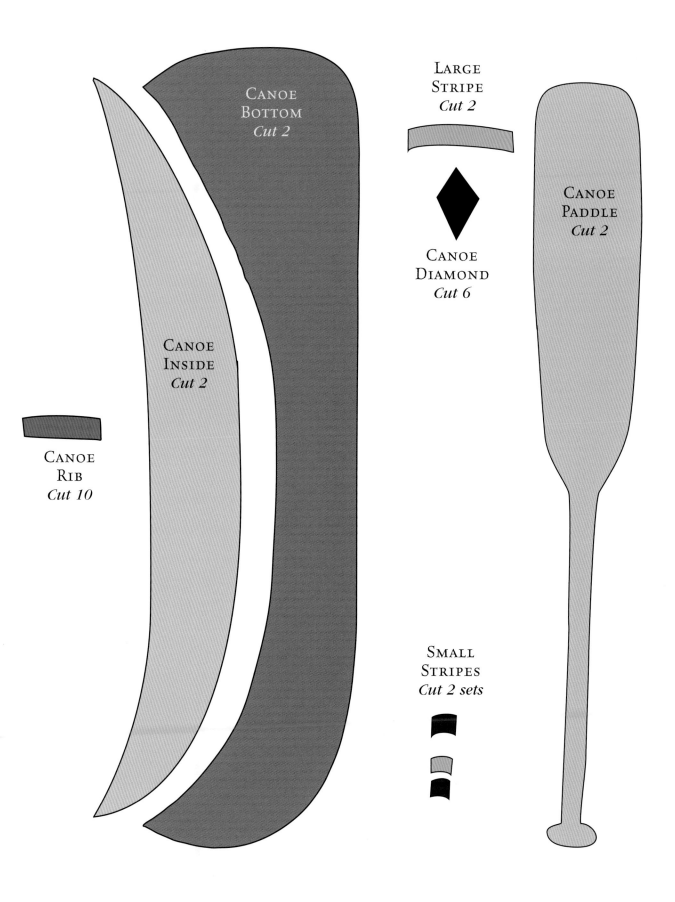

Canoe
Bottom
Cut 2

Large
Stripe
Cut 2

Canoe
Diamond
Cut 6

Canoe
Paddle
Cut 2

Canoe
Inside
Cut 2

Canoe
Rib
Cut 10

Small
Stripes
Cut 2 sets

Quilt it Quick

Crossed Canoes Table Setting

Materials

Finished size is approximately 13" x 19"

Fabrics are based on 42"-wide cotton fabric that has not been washed. Fabric Requirements are for four placemats

1/2 yard cream fabric for centers

3/4 yard of dark red fabric for border and backing

Scraps of gold fabric for canoe paddles

Scraps of red, black, and blue fabric for paddle trims

34" x 46" piece of batting

1-5/8 yard fabric for backing

3/4 yard of black fabric for binding

14" x 14" piece of fusible web for each placemat

Stabilizer for appliqués

Sulky® threads to match appliqué fabrics

Placemats

Cutting Instructions

(A 1/4" seam allowance is included in these measurements.)

• From the cream fabric, cut:
  1 strip 13-1/2" x 42"; from this strip cut:
    4 rectangles 13-1/2" x 7-1/2"

• From the dark red fabric, cut:
  6 strips 3-1/2" x 42"; from these strips cut:
    16 rectangles 3-1/2" x 13-1/2"

• From the black fabric, cut:
  7 strips 2-1/2" x 42" for binding

Assembling the Placemats

1. Sew a dark red 3-1/2" x 13-1/2" rectangle on the top and bottom of each light tan 13-1/2" x 7-1/2" rectangle. Press toward the dark red rectangle. You will need 4 Unit A's.

2. Sew a dark red 3-1/2" x 13-1/2" rectangle on the sides of Unit A. Press toward the dark red rectangle. You will need 4 Unit B's.

3. Trace all appliqué templates from page 31 and cut out.

4. Refer to General Instructions to prepare pieces for appliqué.

5. Use lightweight tear-away stabilizer to machine-appliqué. Place the stabilizer beneath the fabric layers and use a small zigzag stitch to sew around each shape, smoothly covering the raw fabric.

edge. If your machine has stitch options, use them to detail appliqués. After the stitching is complete, remove the stabilizer according to the manufacturer's instructions.

Finishing the Placemats

1. Layer the backing fabric, batting, and placemat top. Baste the layers together.

2. Hand- or machine-quilt as desired.

3. Finish the placemats by sewing on the binding.

Napkins

Materials

Finished size is approximately 17" x 17"

Fabrics are based on 42"-wide cotton fabric that has not been washed. Fabric Requirements are for four placemats

1-1/8" yards of cream fabric

Cutting Instructions

(A 1/4" seam allowance is included in these measurements.)

• From the cream fabric, cut:
  4 squares 18" x 18"

Finishing the Napkins

Sew a narrow, double hem around all four sides of the 4 squares.

Templates for Crossed Canoes Placemats

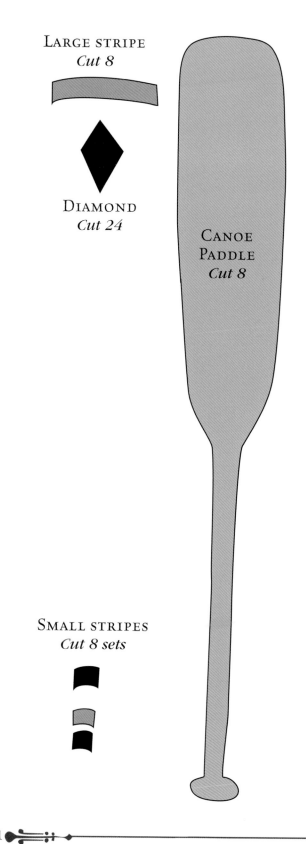

LARGE STRIPE
Cut 8

DIAMOND
Cut 24

CANOE PADDLE
Cut 8

SMALL STRIPES
Cut 8 sets

FLYING GEESE

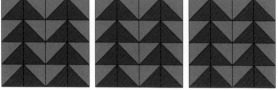

An all-time favorite, the Flying Geese block is featured in a 9-block snuggler with appliqué patterns for an outback cabin and aspen trees for a wilderness wallhanging.

Materials

Finished size is approximately 21" x 21"

Fabrics are based on 42"-wide cotton fabric that has not been washed.

1/2 yard of purple fabric for background

1/2 yard of green fabric for background

1/2 yard of off white for aspen trees

Assorted shades of gold fabric for aspen leaves

Scraps of yellow fabric for windows

Scraps of light brown fabric for logs, cabin roof and cabin edge strip

Scraps of dark brown fabric for chimney and door

1 yard of fusible web

Stabilizer for appliqués

Sulky® threads to match appliqué fabrics

Flying Geese Block

Cutting Instructions

(A 1/4" seam allowance is included in these measurements.)

• From the purple fabric, cut:

  2 strips 6-1/8" x 42"; from these strips, cut:

    8 squares 6-1/8" x 6-1/8"; cut these squares in half diagonally to make 16 half-square triangles

• From the green fabric, cut:

  2 strips 6-1/8" x 42"; from these strips, cut:

    8 squares 6-1/8" x 6-1/8"; cut these squares in half diagonally to make 16 half-square triangles

Assembling the Block

1. Sew the purple 6-1/8" half-square triangles and the green 6-1/8" half-square triangles together. Press toward the green. You will need 16 Unit A's.

Unit A   *Make 16*

2. Sew 2 Unit A's together. Press in the direction of least amount of bulk. You will need 8 Unit B's.

Unit B   *Make 8*

3. Sew 2 Unit B's together. Press in the direction of least amount of bulk. You will need 4 Unit C's.

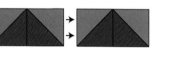 

Unit C   *Make 4*

4. Sew the 4 Unit C's together. Press in the direction of least amount of bulk.

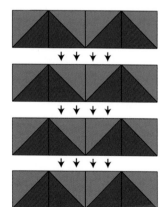 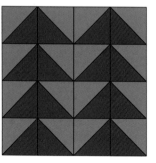

5. Trace all appliqué templates from pages 36-39 and cut out.

6. Refer to General Instructions to prepare pieces for appliqué.

7. Use lightweight tear-away stabilizer to machine appliqué the pieces. Place the stabilizer beneath the fabric layers and use a small zigzag stitch to sew around each shape, smoothly covering the raw fabric edge. If your machine has stitch options, use them to detail the appliqués. After the stitching is complete, remove the stabilizer according to the manufacturer's instructions.

8. Follow the illustration to position remaining appliqué pieces in place on the block. Stitch around the appliqué pieces with a small zigzag stitch to finish rough edges.

Templates for Flying Geese Block

ASPEN TREE
Cut 1

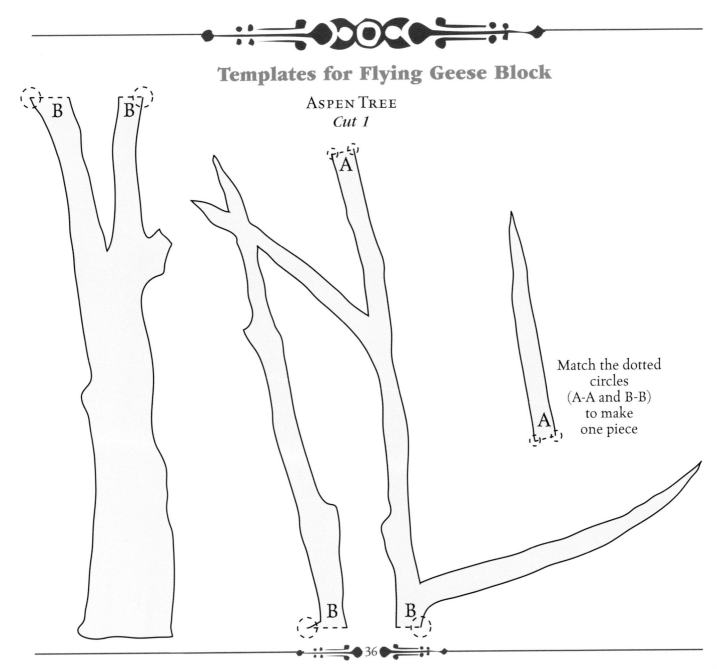

Match the dotted circles (A-A and B-B) to make one piece

Templates for Flying Geese Block

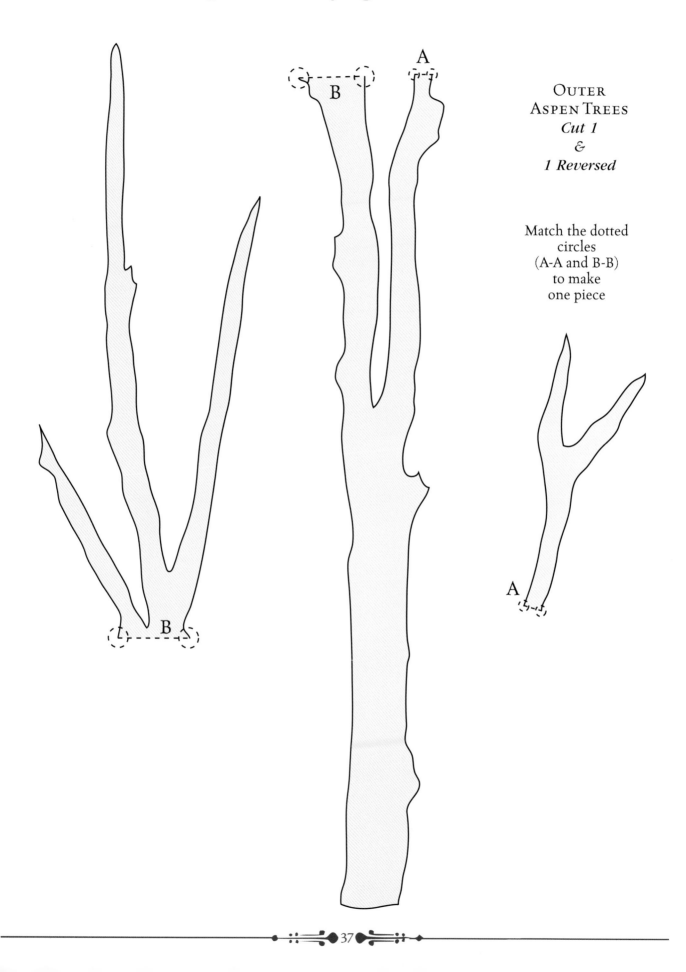

OUTER
ASPEN TREES
Cut 1
&
1 Reversed

Match the dotted
circles
(A-A and B-B)
to make
one piece

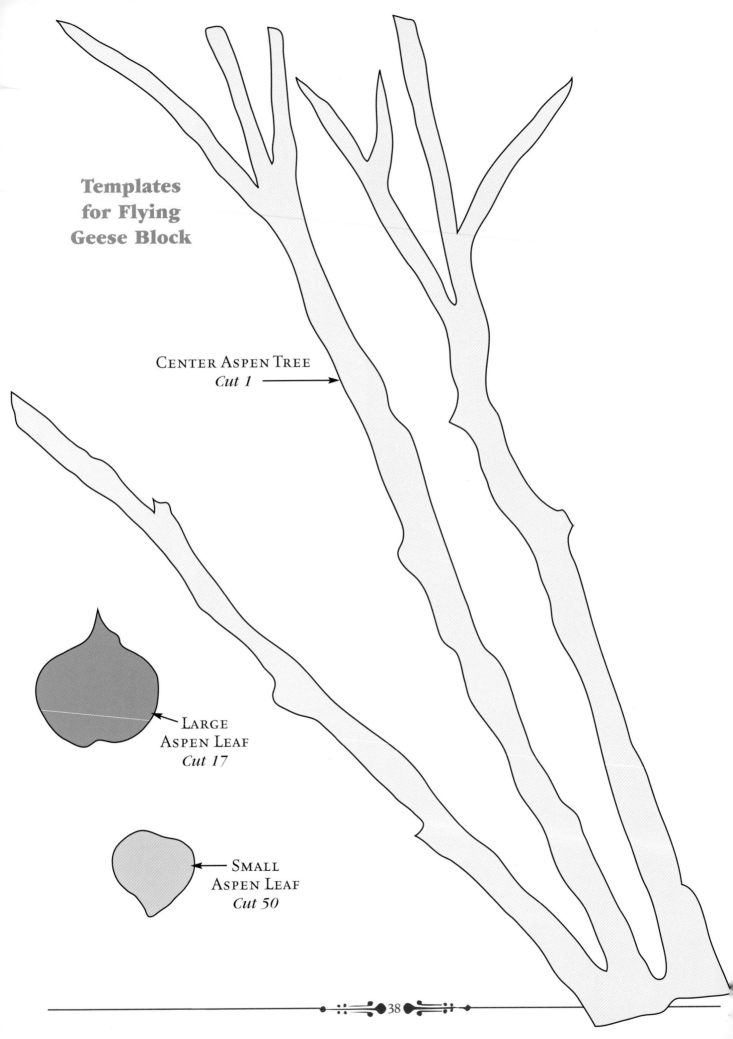

**Templates
for Flying
Geese Block**

CENTER ASPEN TREE
Cut 1

LARGE
ASPEN LEAF
Cut 17

SMALL
ASPEN LEAF
Cut 50

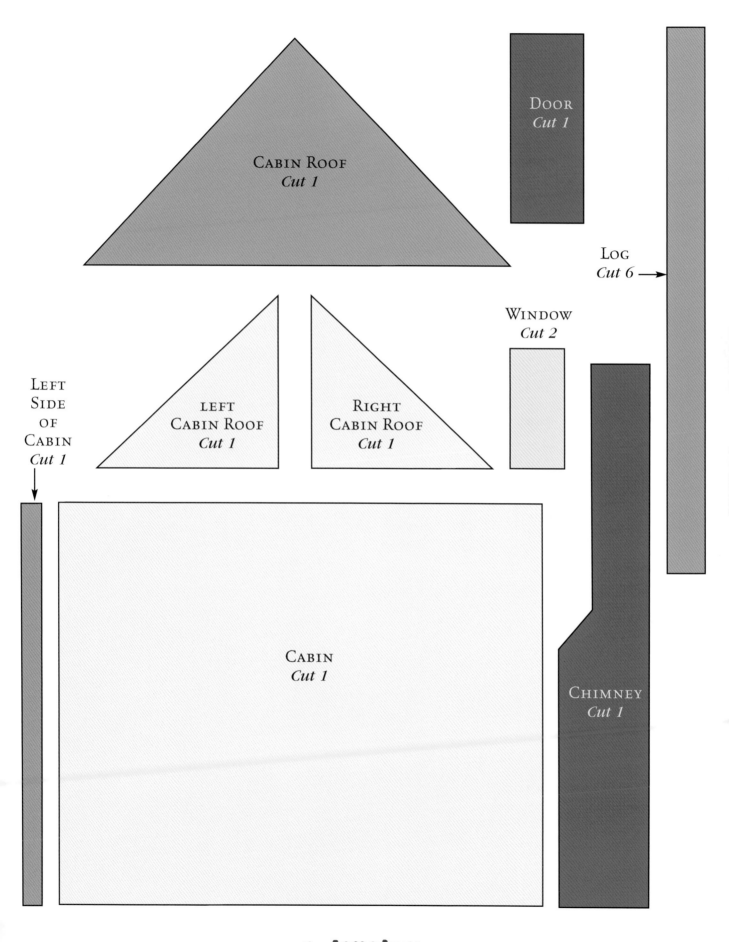

CABIN ROOF
Cut 1

DOOR
Cut 1

LOG
Cut 6 →

LEFT
CABIN ROOF
Cut 1

RIGHT
CABIN ROOF
Cut 1

WINDOW
Cut 2

LEFT
SIDE
OF
CABIN
Cut 1

CABIN
Cut 1

CHIMNEY
Cut 1

Flying Geese Wallhanging

Materials

Finished size is approximately 33" x 33"

Fabrics are based on 42"-wide cotton fabric that has not been washed.

One completed Flying Geese block

Scraps of dark green fabric for corner stones

1/4 yard of cream fabric for sashing

1 yard of medium brown fabric for borders and binding

43" x 43" piece of batting

43" x 43" piece of fabric for backing

Cutting Instructions

- From the dark green fabric, cut:
  1 strip 2-1/2" x 42"; from this strip, cut:
     4 squares 2-1/2" x 2-1/2"

- From the cream fabric cut:
  2 strips 2-1/2" x 42"; from these strips, cut:
     4 rectangles 2-1/2" x 21-1/2"

- From the medium brown fabric, cut:
  4 strips 4-1/2" x 42"
  5 strips 2-1/2" x 42"

Assembling the Wallhanging

1. Sew a dark green 2-1/2" x 2-1/2" square on each of 2 cream 2-1/2" x 21-1/2" rectangles. Press toward the dark. You will have 2 Unit A's.

2. Sew a cream 2-1/2" x 21-1/2" rectangle on each side of the block. Press toward the block. You will have 1 Unit B.

3. Sew Unit A to the top and to the bottom of Unit B. Press in the direction of least amount of bulk.

4. Measure the width of the wallhanging through the center for the top and bottom border measurement. Cut 2 strips that length from the brown 4-1/2"-wide strips. Sew to the top and bottom. Press toward the border.

5. Measure the wallhanging through the center lengthwise for side border measurement. Cut two medium brown strips that length from the 4-1/2"-wide strips. Sew these strips to each side. Press toward the border.

Finishing the Wallhanging

1. Layer the backing fabric, batting, and wallhanging top.

2. Hand- or machine-quilt as desired.

3. Finish the wallhanging by sewing on the binding.

FLYING GEESE SNUGGLER

Materials

Finished size is approximately 62" x 74"

Fabrics are based on 42"-wide fabric that has not been washed.

1-3/4 yards of cream fabric for blocks

■

1-1/8 yards of pale green fabric for blocks and inner border

■

5/8 yard of light green fabric for blocks

■

1-1/8 yards of medium green fabric for blocks and middle border

■

2-1/2 yards of dark green fabric for blocks, outer border and binding

■

1 yard of very dark green for sashing

■

70" x 82" piece of batting

■

5-1/4 yards of fabric for backing

Flying Geese Block

Cutting Instructions

(A 1/4" seam allowance is included in these measurements.)

- From the cream fabric, cut:
  16 strips 3-1/2" x 42"; from these strips, cut:
  192 squares 3-1/2" x 3-1/2"

- From the pale green fabric, cut:
  4 strips 3-1/2" x 42", from these strips, cut:
  24 rectangles 3-1/2" x 6-1/2"
  7 strips 2-1/2" x 42" for inner border

- From the light green fabric, cut:
  4 strips 3-1/2" x 42"; from these strips, cut:
  24 rectangles 3-1/2" x 6-1/2"

- From the medium green fabric, cut:
  4 strips 3-1/2" x 42"; from these strips, cut:
  24 rectangles 3-1/2" x 6-1/2"
  7 strips 2-1/2" x 42" for middle border

- From the dark green fabric, cut:
  4 strips 3-1/2" x 42"; from these strips, cut:
  24 rectangles 3-1/2" x 6-1/2"
  7 strips 5-1/2" x 42" for outer border
  7 strips 3" x 42" for binding

- From the very dark green fabric, cut:
  12 strips 2-1/2" x 42"; from 3 of these strips, cut:
  3 strips into 8 rectangles 2-1/2" x 12-1/2"
  Set aside remaining strips for sashing

Assembling the Block

1. On the wrong side of the 192 cream 3-1/2" x 3-1/2" background squares, draw a diagonal line.

2. Place a 3-1/2" cream square on the right side of the 24 pale green 3-1/2" x 6-1/2" rectangles. Sew on the drawn line. Press the 3-1/2" square toward the outside. Trim away the middle triangle only, leaving a 1/4" seam allowance past the sewing line. You will need 24 Unit A's.

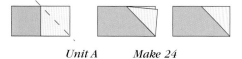

Unit A   Make 24

3. Place a 3-1/2" cream square on the left side of Unit A. Sew on the drawn line. Press the 3-1/2" square toward the outside. Trim away the middle triangle only, leaving a 1/4" seam allowance past sewing line. You will need 24 Unit B's.

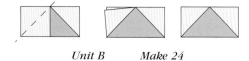

Unit B   Make 24

4. Repeat steps 2 and 3 using the 24 light green rectangles, 24 medium green rectangles, and the 24 dark green rectangles.

Unit C   Unit D   Unit E
Light Green   Medium Green   Dark Green
Make 24   Make 24   Make 24

5. Sew 2 Unit B's together. Press in the direction of least amount of bulk. You will have 12 Unit F's.

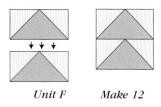

Unit F   Make 12

6. Repeat step 5 with the light green Unit C's, the medium green Unit D's, and the dark green Unit E's.

Unit G   Unit H   Unit I
Light Green   Medium Green   Dark Green
Make 12   Make 12   Make 12

7. Sew medium green Unit H and pale green Unit F together. Press in the direction of least amount of bulk. You will have 12 Unit J's.

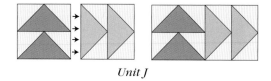

Unit J

8. Sew light green Unit G and dark green Unit I together. Press in the direction of least amount of bulk. You will have 12 Unit K's.

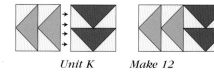

Unit K   Make 12

9. Sew Unit J and Unit K together. Press in the direction of least amount of bulk. You will have 12 Unit L's.

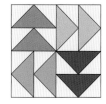

Unit L   Make 12

Adding the Sashing

1. Sew 2 very dark green 2-1/2" x 12-1/2" rectangles and 3 Unit L's together. Press in the direction of least amount of bulk. You will have 4 rows total.

2. Measure a row through the center for sashing strip measurement. Cut 5 very dark green 2-1/2" strips to that length.

3. Sew the strips and rows together. Press in the direction of least amount of bulk.

4. Measure the length of the quilt top through the center for the side sashing measurement. Cut 2 very dark green 2-1/2" strips that length. Sew a strip to each side. Press toward the sashing.

Adding the Borders

1. Measure the width of the quilt top through the center for the inner border measurement. Cut 2 pale green 2-1/2" strips to that length. Sew the strips to the top and bottom of quilt top. Press toward the border.

2. Measure the length of the quilt top through the center for inner border measurement. Cut 2 pale green 2-1/2" strips to that length. Sew to each side of quilt top. Press toward the border.

3. Repeat steps 1 and 2 for the medium green middle border and the dark green outer border.

Finishing the Quilt

1. Layer the backing fabric, batting, and the top.

2. Baste the layers together. Hand or machine quilt as desired.

3. Finish the quilt by sewing on the binding.

Flying Geese Snuggler

BEAR PAW

Make the Bear Paw block your catch
of the day featured on a 24-block
snuggler with appliqué patterns for a
bear bath set complete with bear tracks
stenciled on a cotton rug.

BEAR PAW BLOCK

Materials

Finished size is approximately 21" x 21"

Fabrics are based on 42"-wide cotton fabric that has not been washed.

3/4 yard of tan fabric for block

■

1/2 yard of dark blue fabric for block

■

1/2 yard of golden brown fabric for block

■

Scrap of dark black-and-brown fabric for bear's body

■

Scrap of light brown fabric for bear's nose, inside of the paw prints, and stones

■

Scrap of tan fabric for bear's muzzle

■

Scrap of black fabric for paw prints, claws, and tip of bear's nose

■

Scrap of blue fabric for water splashes

■

Scrap of medium green fabric for 2 pines and fish

■

Scrap of dark green fabric for pine tree

■

Scrap of medium brown fabric for pine tree trunks and stones

■

Scrap of off-white fabric for aspen tree trunk

■

3/4 yard of fusible web

■

Stabilizer for appliqués

■

Sulky® threads to match appliqué fabrics

Bear Paw Block

Cutting Instructions

(A 1/4" seam allowance is included in these measurements.)

• From the tan fabric, cut:
  1 strip 4-1/4" x 42"; from this strip, cut:
    1 square 4-1/4" x 4-1/4"
  1 strip 4-5/8" x 42"; from this strip, cut:
    3 squares 4-5/8" x 4-5/8", cut squares in half diagonally once to make 6 half-square triangles
  1 strip 11-1/2" x 42"; from this strip, cut:
    2 squares 11-1/2" x 11-1/2", cut squares in half diagonally once to make 4 half-square triangles

• From the dark blue fabric, cut:
  1 strip 4-5/8" x 42"; from this strip, cut:
    3 squares 4-5/8" x 4-5/8"; cut squares in half diagonally once to make 6 half-square triangles
  1 strip 12-1/8" x 42"; from this strip, cut:
    1 square 12-1/8" x 12-1/8"; cut square in half diagonally once to make 2 half-square triangles
  (Note: 1 triangle will not be used)

• From the golden brown fabric, cut:
  1 strip 12-1/8" x 42"; from this strip, cut:
    1 square 12-1/8" x 12-1/8"; cut square in half diagonally once to make 2 half-square triangles
  (Note: 1 triangle will not be used)

Assembling the Block

1. Sew the dark blue 4-5/8" half-square triangles and the tan 4-5/8" half-square triangles together. Press toward the dark blue. You will have 6 Unit A's.

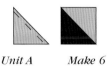

Unit A   Make 6

2. Sew 3 Unit A's together, exactly as shown. Press toward the dark blue. You will have 1 Unit B.

Unit B   Make 1

3. Sew 3 Unit A's together, exactly as shown. Press toward the dark blue. You will have 1 Unit C.

Unit C   *Make 1*

4. Sew the tan 4-1/4" square to Unit B on the left side. Press toward the square. You will have 1 Unit D.

 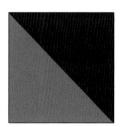

Unit D   *Make 1*

5. Sew a golden brown 12-1/8" half-square triangle and a dark blue 12-1/8" half-square triangle together. Press toward the dark blue. You will have 1 Unit E.

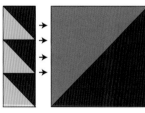 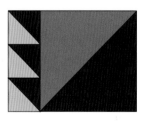

Unit E   *Make 1*

6. Sew Unit C to the left side of Unit E. Press toward the square. You will have 1 Unit F.

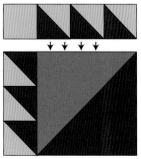 

Unit F   *Make 1*

7. Sew Unit D to the top of Unit F. Press toward the square. You will have 1 Unit G.

Unit G   *Make 1*

8. Sew 2 tan 11-1/2" half-square triangles to opposite sides of Unit G. Press toward the triangle.

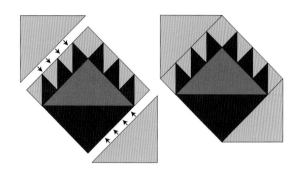

9. Sew the 2 remaining 11-1/2" half-square triangles to the remaining sides of Unit G. Press toward the tan triangle.

 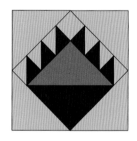

10. Square up the block, if necessary. Leave a 1/4" seam allowance past the intersection and make sure that the corners are at 90° angles.

Adding the Appliqués

1. Trace all appliqué templates from pages 51-53 and cut out.

2. Refer to General Instructions to prepare pieces for appliqué.

3. Use lightweight tear-away stabilizer to machine-appliqué the pieces. Place the stabilizer beneath the fabric layers and use a small zigzag stitch to sew around each shape, smoothly covering the raw fabric edge. If your machine has stitch options, use them to detail the appliqués. After the stitching is complete, remove the stabilizer according to the manufacturer's instructions.

Templates for Bear Paw Block

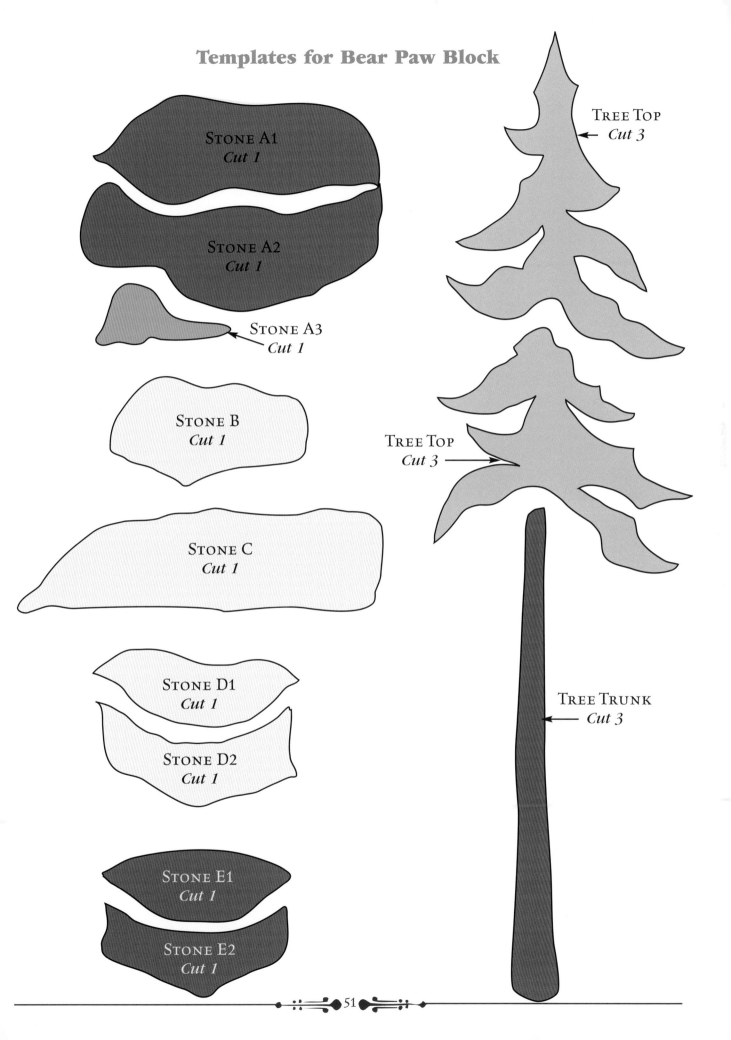

Stone A1
Cut 1

Stone A2
Cut 1

Stone A3
Cut 1

Stone B
Cut 1

Stone C
Cut 1

Stone D1
Cut 1

Stone D2
Cut 1

Stone E1
Cut 1

Stone E2
Cut 1

Tree Top
Cut 3

Tree Top
Cut 3

Tree Trunk
Cut 3

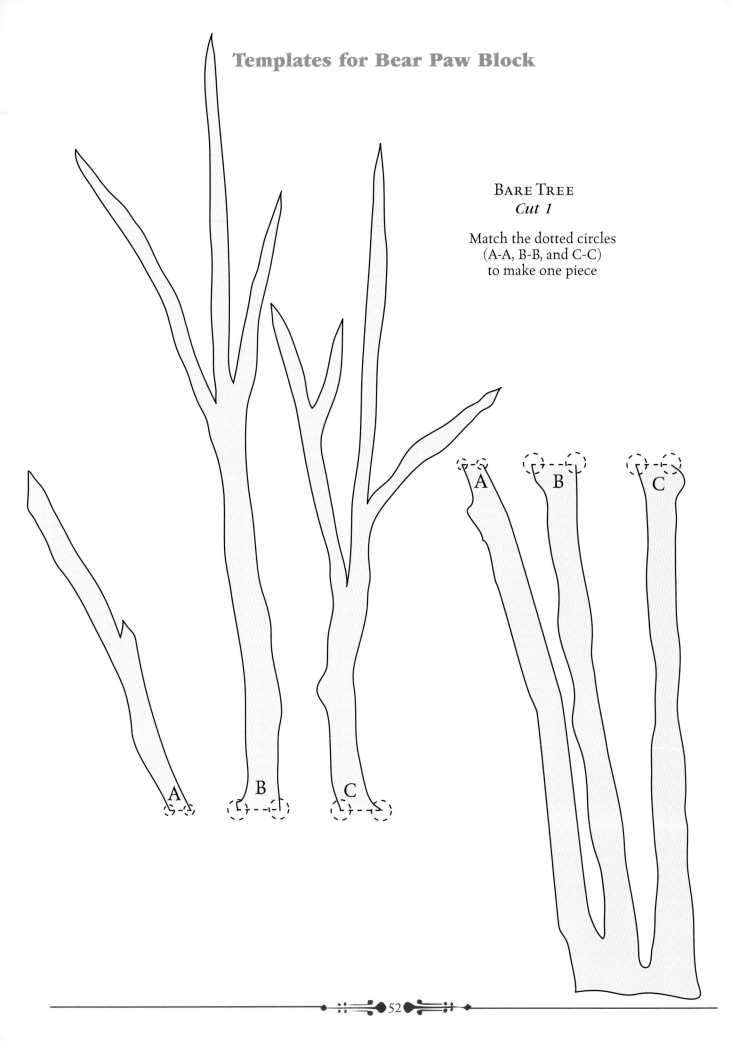

BARE TREE
Cut 1

Match the dotted circles
(A-A, B-B, and C-C)
to make one piece

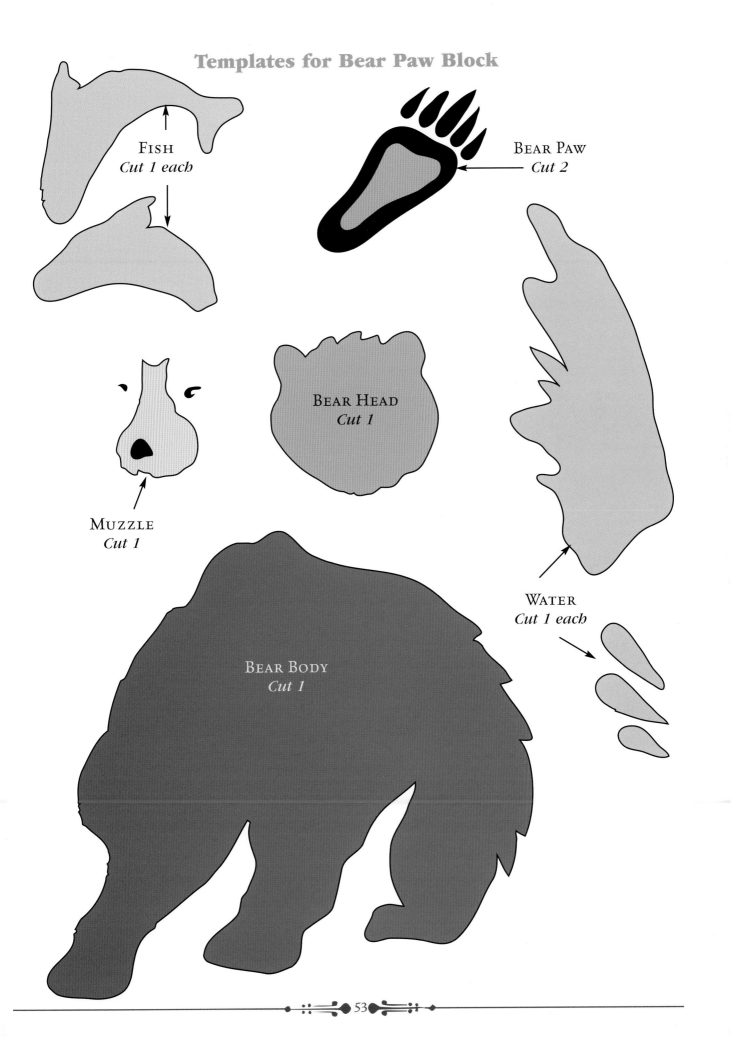

Templates for Bear Paw Block

FISH
Cut 1 each

BEAR PAW
Cut 2

MUZZLE
Cut 1

BEAR HEAD
Cut 1

WATER
Cut 1 each

BEAR BODY
Cut 1

Bear Paw Snuggler

Materials

Finished size is approximately 61" x 85"

Fabrics are based on 42"-wide cotton fabric that has not been washed.

3-3/4 yards of dark blue fabric for blocks, outer border and binding

■

1 yard of golden brown fabric for blocks

■

1-5/8 yards of cream fabric for sashing

■

1/4 yard of black fabric for cornerstones

■

69" x 93" piece of batting

■

5-1/2 yards of fabric for backing

Bear Paw Block

Make 24

Cutting Instructions

(A 1/4" seam allowance is included in these measurements.)

- From the dark blue fabric, cut:

  4 strips 6-1/2" x 42"; from these strips, cut:

  24 squares 6-1/2" x 6-1/2"

  5 strips 3-7/8" x 42"; from these strips, cut:

  48 squares 3-7/8" x 3-7/8"; cut squares in half diagonally to make 96 half-square triangles

  1 strip 3-1/2" x 42"; from this strip, cut:

  6 squares 3-1/2" x 3-1/2"

  8 strips 5-1/2" x 42" for the outer border

  7 strips 3" x 42" for binding

- From the golden brown fabric, cut:

  2 strips 3-1/2" x 42"; from these strips, cut:

  24 squares 3-1/2" x 3-1/2"

  5 strips 3-7/8" x 42"; from this strip, cut:

  48 squares 3-7/8" x 3-7/8"; cut squares in half diagonally to make 96 half-square triangles

- From the cream fabric, cut:

  6 strips 3-1/2" x 42"; from these strips, cut:

  24 rectangles 3-1/2" x 9-1/2"

  9 strips 3-1/2" x 42"; from this strip, cut:

  17 rectangles 3-1/2" x 21-1/2"

- From the black fabric, cut:

  1 strip 3-1/2" x 42"; from these strips, cut:

  12 squares 3-1/2" x 3-1/2"

Assembling the Block

1. Sew the 96 dark blue 3-7/8" triangles and 96 golden brown 3-7/8" triangles together. Press toward the dark. You will have 96 Unit A's.

Unit A   *Make 96*

2. Using half the Unit A's, sew 2 Unit A's together, exactly as shown. Press toward the dark. You will have 24 Unit B's.

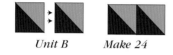

Unit B   *Make 24*

3. Using the remaining Unit A's, sew 2 Unit A's together, exactly as shown. Press toward the dark blue. You will have 24 Unit C's.

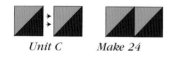

Unit C   *Make 24*

4. Sew a golden brown 3-1/2" square to each Unit B on the left side. Press toward the square. You will have 24 Unit D's.

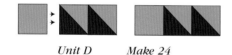

Unit D   *Make 24*

5. Sew Unit C to the left side of a dark blue 6-1/2" square. Press toward the square. You will need 24 Unit E's.

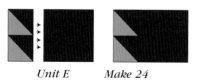

Unit E   *Make 24*

6. Sew Unit D to the top of Unit E, as shown. Press toward the square. You will need 24 Unit F's.

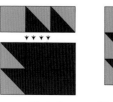

Unit F   *Make 24*

Adding the Sashing

1. Sew a dark blue 3-1/2" square and 2 cream 3-1/2" x 9-1/2" rectangles together. Press toward the cream rectangles. You will need 6 Unit G's.

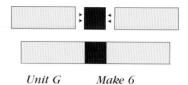

Unit G   *Make 6*

2. Sew a cream 3-1/2" x 9-1/2" rectangle and 2 Unit F's together. Press towards the cream rectangle. You will have 12 Unit H's.

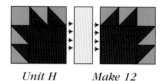

Unit H   *Make 12*

3. Sew a Unit G and 2 Unit H's together. Press in the direction of the least amount of bulk. You will have 6 Unit I's.

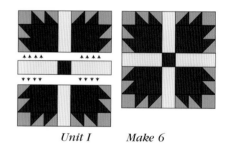

Unit I   *Make 6*

4. Sew 2 cream 3-1/2" x 21-1/2" rectangles, and 2 Unit I's together. Press towards the cream rectangles. You will need 3 Unit J's.

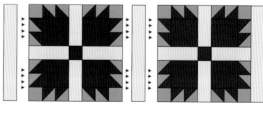

Unit J   *Make 3*

5. Sew 2 cream 3-1/2" x 21-1/2" rectangles and 3 black 3-1/2" squares together. Press toward the cream. You will have 4 Unit K's.

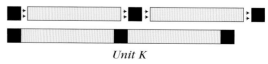

Unit K

6. Sew a Unit K to the top of each Unit J. Sew the remaining Unit K to the bottom of Unit J.

Adding the Borders

1. Measure the width of the quilt top through the center to get the top and bottom border measurement. Cut 2 strips to that length from the dark blue 5-1/2" strips. Sew to the top and bottom of the quilt. Press toward the border.

2. Measure the length of the quilt top through the top to get the side border measurement. Cut 2 strips to that length from the dark blue 5-1/2" strips. Sew a strip to each side of the quilt top. Press toward the border.

Finishing the Quilt

1. Layer the quilt backing fabric, batting, and quilt top. Baste the layers together.

2. Hand- or machine-quilt as desired.

3. Finish the quilt by sewing on the binding.

Bear Paw Snuggler

Quilt it Quick
Bear Bath Set

Materials

Bath and Hand Towel

Purchased bath and hand towel

■

1/4 yard of black fabric for
bears' bodies, tip of nose and paw prints

■

6" x 6" piece of brown fabric for bears' heads

■

4" x 4" piece of tan fabric for bears' noses

■

8" x 8" piece of green fabric for trees

■

Stabilizer

■

3/4 yard of fusible web

■

Sulky® threads to match appliqués

Stenciled Rug

Purchased cotton rug

■

Black permanent marker

■

Black acrylic paint

■

Stencil brush

■

1 sheet of template plastic

■

Art knife

Adding the Appliqués

1. Trace all appliqué templates from page 59 and cut out.

2. Refer to General Instructions to prepare pieces for appliqué.

3. Use lightweight tear-away stabilizer to machine-appliqué the pieces. Place the stabilizer beneath the fabric layers and use a small zigzag stitch to sew around each shape, smoothly covering the raw fabric edge. If your machine has stitch options, use them to detail the appliqués. After the stitching is complete, remove the stabilizer according to the manufacturer's instructions.

Stenciled Bear Tracks Rug

1. With a black permanent marker, trace one pair of bear paw prints onto template plastic. Paws can be arranged unevenly to resemble a bear walking.

2. Cut out within the traced lines with the art knife. Try to cut as smoothly as possible to avoid jagged edges.

3. Place a piece of cardboard under rug before starting. Pour a small amount of black paint into a tray. Dip stencil brush into the paint. Dab once on a piece of paper towel to eliminate excess paint. Stencil with a dabbing motion inside cut-out parts of template.

4. When complete, carefully lift template off the rug and wait for the paint to dry thoroughly.

5. Move template forward and stencil another pair of tracks.

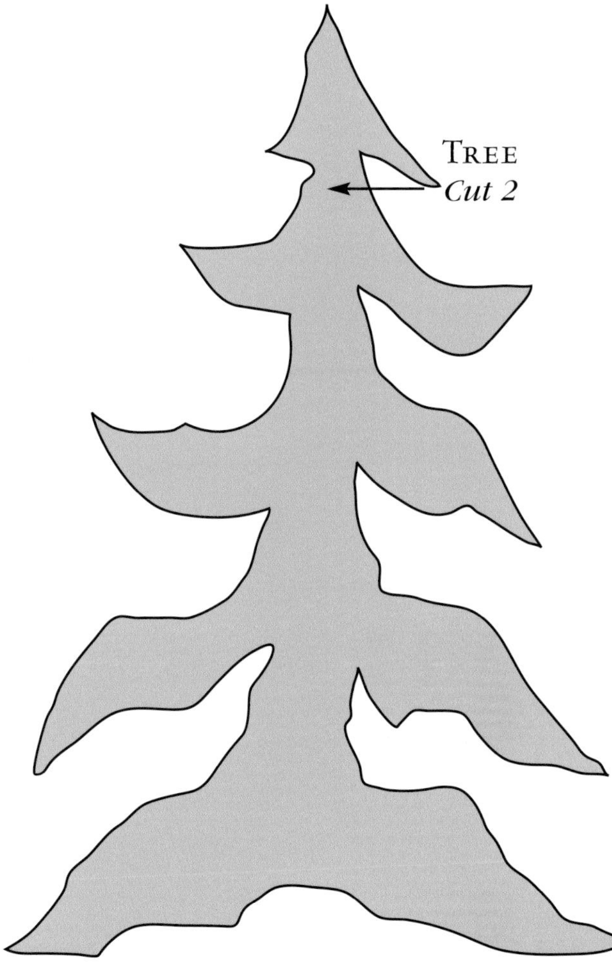

TREE
Cut 2

PAW PRINT
(APPLIQUÉ)
Cut 4

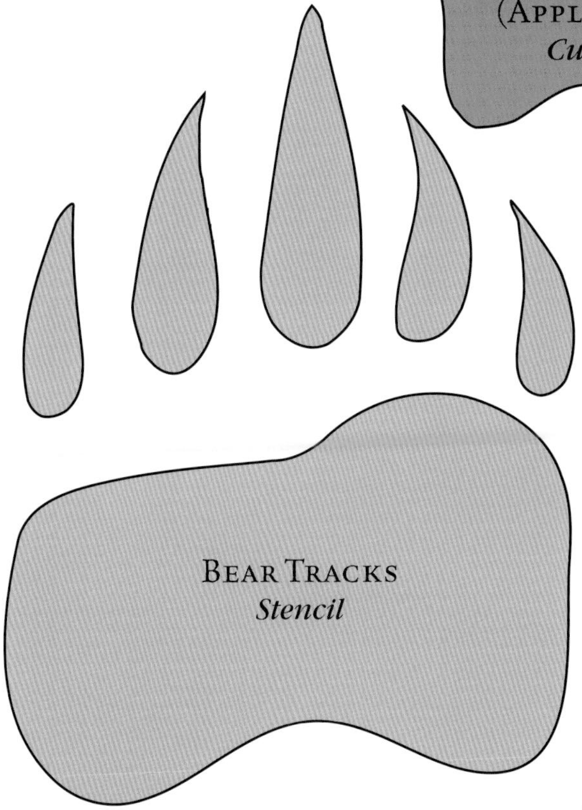

BEAR TRACKS
Stencil

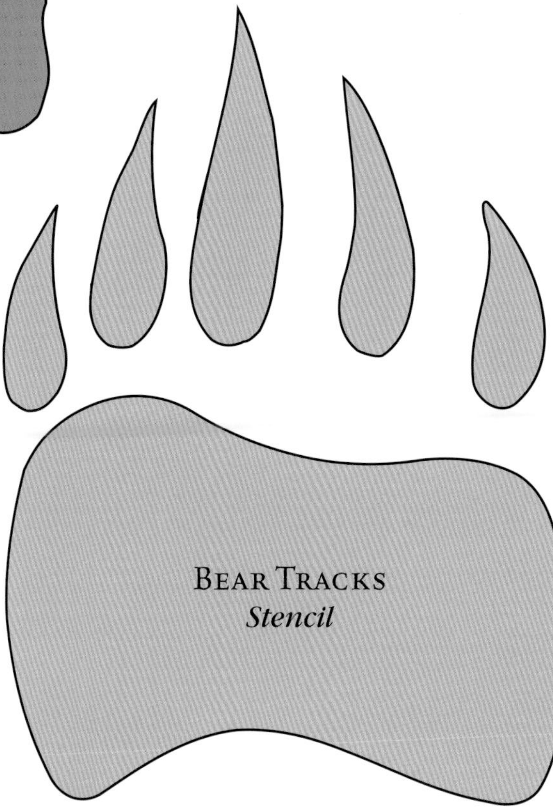

BEAR TRACKS
Stencil

Log Cabin Block

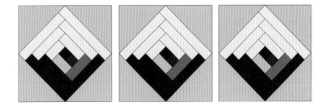

The Log Cabin block set on point is an easy way to build a stunning 6-block snuggler and the perfect background to appliqué a lonely loon and lilies on a waterfowl wallhanging and bath set.

Materials

Finished size is approximately 21" x 21"

Fabrics are based on 42" wide cotton fabric that has not been washed.

1/4 yard of cream fabric for background

5/8 yard sky blue fabric for background

1/6 yard of dark blue fabric for background

1/6 yard of royal blue fabric for background

1/6 yard of medium blue fabric for background

1/4 yard total of 3 assorted green fabrics for lily pads

Scrap of off-white fabric for clouds

Scrap of black fabric for loon body and head

Scrap of white fabric for loon neck and lily buds

Scrap of pale yellow fabric for lilies

Scrap of gold fabric for lily centers

1 yard of fusible web

Stabilizer for appliqués

Sulky® threads to match appliqué fabrics

Log Cabin Block

Cutting Instructions

(A 1/4" seam allowance is included in these measurements.)

• From the cream fabric, cut:
  2 strips 2-5/8" x 42"; from these strips, cut:
      1 rectangle 2-5/8" x 4-3/4"
      1 rectangle 2-5/8" x 6-7/8"
      1 rectangle 2-5/8" x 9"
      1 rectangle 2-5/8" x 11-1/8"
      1 rectangle 2-5/8" x 13-1/4"
      1 rectangle 2-5/8" x 15-3/8"

• From the sky blue fabric, cut:
  1 strip 2-5/8" x 42"; from this strip, cut:
      1 rectangle 2-5/8" x 4-3/4"
  1 strip 11-1/2" x 42"; from this strip, cut:
      2 squares 11-1/2" x 11-1/2"; cut squares in half diagonally to make 4 half-square triangles

• From the royal blue fabric, cut:
  1 strip 2-5/8" x 42"; from this strip, cut:
      1 square 2-5/8" x 2-5/8"
      1 rectangle 2-5/8" x 11-1/8"
      1 rectangle 2-5/8" x 13-1/4"

• From the medium blue fabric, cut:
  1 strip 2-5/8" x 42"; from this strip, cut:
      1 rectangle 2-5/8" x 6-7/8"

• From the dark blue fabric, cut:
  1 strip 2-5/8" x 42"; from this strip, cut:
      1 square 2-5/8" x 2-5/8"
      1 rectangle 2-5/8" x 9"

Assembling the Block

1. Sew a dark blue 2-5/8" square and a bright blue 2-5/8" square together. Press toward the dark blue. Square up the block, if necessary. You will have 1 Unit A.

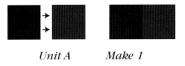

Unit A   Make 1

2. Sew a sky blue 2-5/8" x 4-3/4" rectangle to Unit A, as shown. Press toward the light blue. Square up the block, if necessary. You will have 1 Unit B.

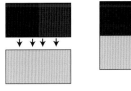

Unit B   Make 1

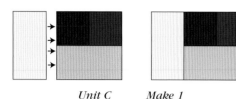

3. Sew a cream 2-5/8" x 4-3/4" rectangle to Unit B. Press toward the cream. Square up the block, if necessary. You will have 1 Unit C.

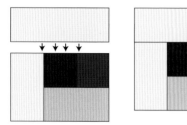

Unit C   *Make 1*

4. Sew a cream 2-5/8" x 6-7/8" rectangle to Unit C. Press toward the cream. Square up the block, if necessary. You will have 1 Unit D.

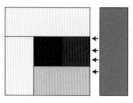

Unit D   *Make 1*

5. Sew a medium blue 2-5/8" x 6-7/8" rectangle to Unit D. Press toward the medium blue. Square up the block, if necessary. You will have 1 Unit E.

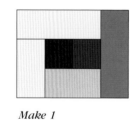

Unit E   *Make 1*

6. Sew a dark blue 2-5/8" x 9" rectangle to Unit E. Press toward the dark blue. Square up the block, if necessary. You will have 1 Unit F.

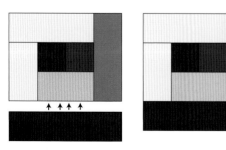

Unit F   *Make 1*

7. Sew a cream 2-5/8" x 9" rectangle to Unit F. Press toward the cream. Square up the block, if necessary. You will have 1 Unit G.

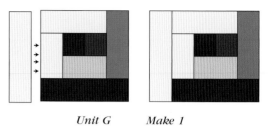

Unit G   *Make 1*

8. Sew a cream 2-5/8" x 11-1/8" rectangle to Unit G. Press toward the cream. Square up the block, if necessary. You will have 1 Unit H.

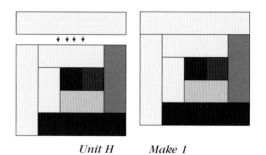

Unit H   *Make 1*

9. Sew a royal blue 2-5/8" x 11-1/8" rectangle to Unit H. Press toward the royal blue. Square up the block, if necessary. You will have 1 Unit I.

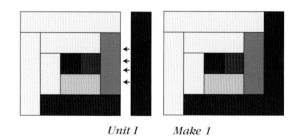

Unit I   *Make 1*

10. Sew a royal blue 2-5/8" x 13-1/4" rectangle to Unit I. Press toward the royal blue. Square up the block, if necessary. You will have 1 Unit J.

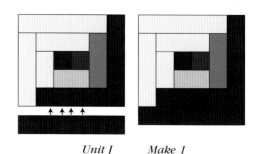

Unit J   *Make 1*

11. Sew a cream 2-5/8" x 13-1/4" rectangle to Unit J. Press toward the cream. Square up the block, if necessary. You will have 1 Unit K.

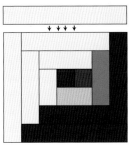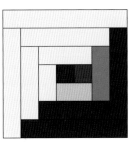

Unit K   *Make 1*

12. Sew a cream 2-5/8" x 15-3/8" rectangle to Unit K. Press toward the cream. Square up the block, if necessary. You will have 1 Unit L.

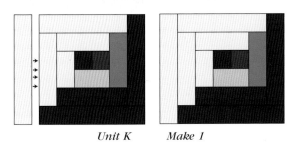

Unit L   *Make 1*

13. Sew the sky blue 11-1/2" half-square triangle to opposite sides of the block, as shown. Press carefully toward the triangles.

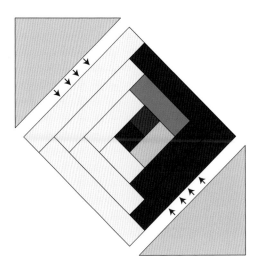

14. Sew sky blue 11-1/2" half-square triangles to the remaining two sides of the block, as shown. Press carefully toward the triangle. Square up the block, if necessary. Make sure to leave a 1/4" seam allowance past the intersections and make sure that the corners are at 90° angles.

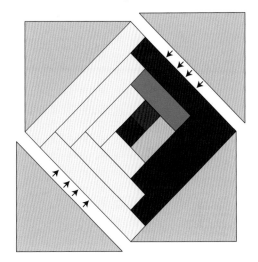

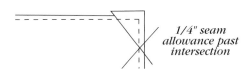

1/4" seam allowance past intersection

Adding the Appliqués

1. Trace all appliqué templates from pages 66-67 and cut out.

2. Refer to General Instructions to prepare pieces for appliqué.

3. Use lightweight tear-away stabilizer to machine appliqué the pieces. Place the stabilizer beneath the fabric layers and use a small zigzag stitch to sew around each shape, smoothly covering the raw fabric edge. If your machine has stitch options, use them to detail the appliqués. After the stitching is complete, remove the stabilizer according to the manufacturer's instructions.

Templates for Log Cabin Block

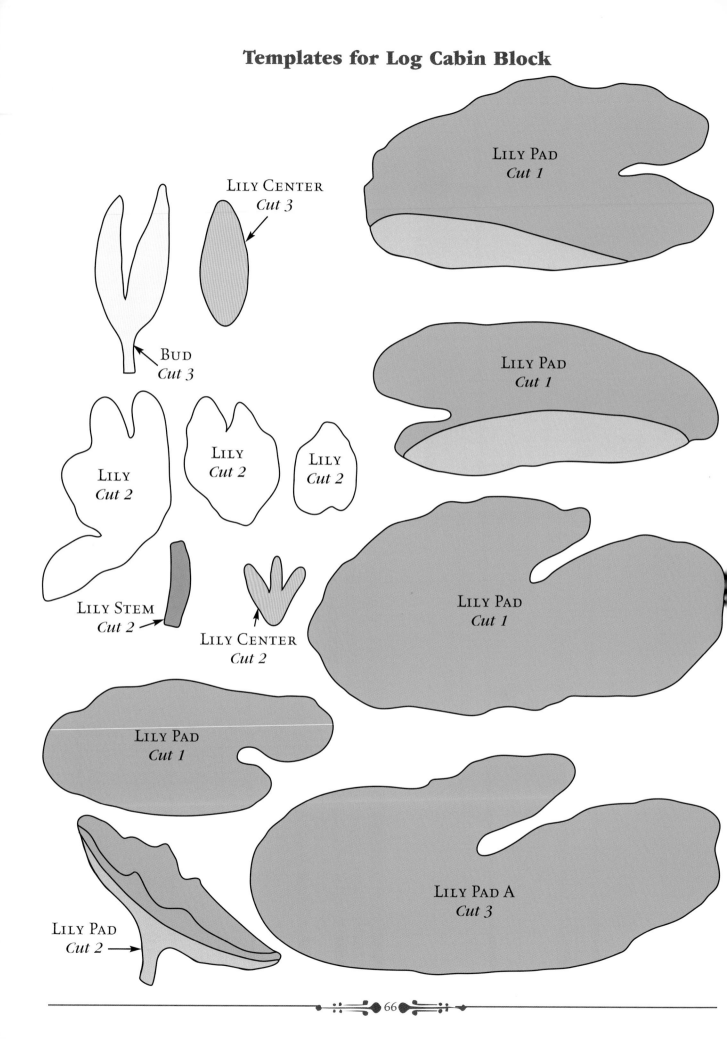

LILY PAD
Cut 1

LILY CENTER
Cut 3

BUD
Cut 3

LILY PAD
Cut 1

LILY
Cut 2

LILY
Cut 2

LILY
Cut 2

LILY PAD
Cut 1

LILY STEM
Cut 2

LILY CENTER
Cut 2

LILY PAD
Cut 1

LILY PAD A
Cut 3

LILY PAD
Cut 2

Templates for Log Cabin Block

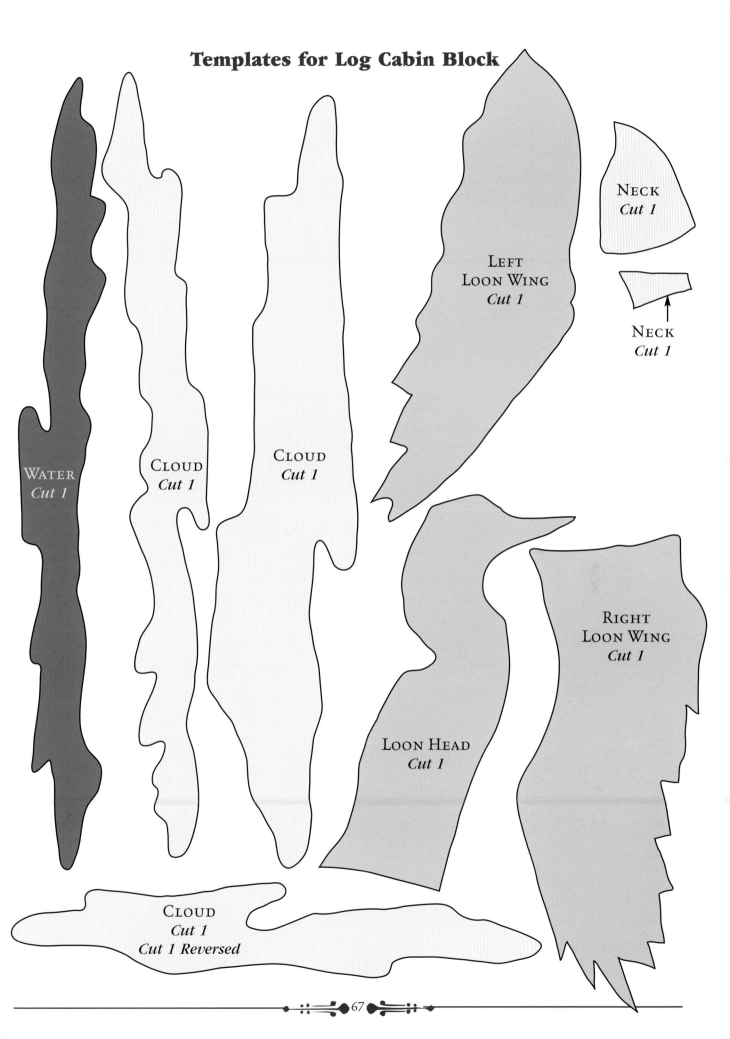

WATER
Cut 1

CLOUD
Cut 1

CLOUD
Cut 1

LEFT LOON WING
Cut 1

NECK
Cut 1

NECK
Cut 1

RIGHT LOON WING
Cut 1

LOON HEAD
Cut 1

CLOUD
Cut 1
Cut 1 Reversed

Log Cabin Wallhanging

Materials

Finished size is approximately 33" x 33"

Fabrics are based on 42"-wide cotton fabric that has not been washed.

One completed Log Cabin Block
■
Scraps of medium blue fabric for cornerstones
■
1/3 yard of cream fabric for sashing
■
1 yard of royal blue fabric for borders and binding
■
43" x 43" piece of batting
■
43" x 43" piece of fabric for backing

Cutting Instructions

• From the medium blue fabric, cut:
   4 squares 2-1/2" x 2-1/2" for cornerstones

• From the cream fabric, cut:
   4 strips 2-1/2" x 42"; from these strips, cut:
      4 rectangles 2-1/2" x 21-1/2"

• From the royal blue fabric, cut:
   4 strips 4-1/2" x 42"
   5 strips 2-1/2" x 42"

Assembling the Wallhanging

1. Sew a medium blue 2-1/2" x 2-1/2" square on each of 2 cream 2-1/2" x 21-1/2" rectangles. Press toward the blue. You will have two Unit A's.

2. Sew a cream 2-1/2" x 21-1/2" rectangle on each side of the block. Press toward the block. You will have one Unit B.

3. Sew Unit A to the top and bottom of Unit B. Press in the direction of least amount of bulk.

4. Measure the width of the wallhanging through the center to get top and bottom border measurement. Cut two strips to that length from the royal blue 4-1/2" wide strips. Sew strips to the top and bottom. Press toward the border.

5. Measure the length of the wallhanging through the center for side border measurement. Cut two royal blue strips to that length from the 4-1/2"-wide strips. Sew to each side. Press toward the border.

Finishing the Wallhanging

1. Layer the backing fabric, batting, and top.

2. Hand- or machine-quilt as desired.

3. Finish the wallhanging by sewing on the binding.

Lonely Loon Bath Set

Materials

Purchased bath, hand towel, and washcloth set

■

9" x 9" piece of black fabric for loon body

■

5" x 5" piece of white fabric
for lily buds and loon neck

■

4" x 9" piece of medium blue fabric for water

■

4" x 4" piece of pale yellow fabric for lily centers

■

8" x 8" piece of light green fabric for lily pads

■

6" x 6" piece of dark green fabric for lily pads

■

1/2 yard fusible web

■

Stabilizer

■

Sulky® threads to match appliqués

Adding the Appliqués

1. Trace appliqué templates from pages 66-67 and cut out.

2. Refer to General Instructions to prepare pieces for appliqué.

3. Use lightweight tear-away stabilizer to machine-appliqué the pieces. Place the stabilizer beneath the fabric layers and use a small zigzag stitch to sew around each shape, smoothly covering the raw fabric edge. If your machine has stitch options, use them to detail the appliqués. After the stitching is complete, remove the stabilizer according to the manufacturer's instructions.

LOG CABIN SNUGGLER

Materials

Finished size is approximately 60" x 81"

Yardage is based on 40"-wide flannel fabric that has not been washed.

7/8 yard of navy blue flannel
for blocks and triangles

3/8 yard of bright blue flannel for blocks

1/4 yard of light blue flannel for blocks

7/8 yard of rust flannel for blocks and triangles

1/2 yard of tan flannel for blocks

1/3 yard of cocoa flannel for blocks

1/3 yard of medium blue flannel for blocks

1/2 yard of green flannel for triangles

3 yards of gold flannel for blocks, triangles,
the outer border, and the binding

1/2 yard of green flannel for triangles

7/8 yard of dark green flannel for the inner border

A 68" x 89" piece of batting

5-1/2 yards of flannel for backing

Log Cabin Block

Make 6 blocks

Cutting instructions

(Measurements include a 1/4" seam allowance)

- From the navy blue flannel, cut:
  4 strips 2-5/8" x 40"; from these strips, cut:
    6 squares 2-5/8" x 2-5/8"
    6 rectangles 2-5/8" x 6-7/8"
    6 rectangles 2-5/8" x 13-1/4"
  1 strip 11-1/2" x 40"; from this strip, cut:
    3 squares 11-1/2"x 11-1/2"; cut each square
    diagonally to make 6 half-square triangles

- From the bright blue flannel, cut:
  3 strips 2-5/8" x 40"; from these strips, cut:
    6 squares 2-5/8" x 2-5/8"
    6 rectangles 2-5/8" x 9"

- From the light blue flannel, cut:
  1 strip 2-5/8" x 40"; from this strip, cut:
    6 rectangles 2-5/8" x 4-3/4"

- From the rust flannel, cut:
  4 strips 2-5/8" x 40"; from these strips, cut:
    6 rectangles 2-5/8" x 4-3/4"
    6 rectangles 2-5/8" x 15-3/8"
  1 strip 11-1/2" x 40"; from this strip, cut:
    3 squares 11-1/2" x 11-1/2"; cut each square
    diagonally to make 6 half-square triangles

- From the tan flannel, cut:
  4 strips 2-5/8" x 40"; from these strips, cut:
    6 rectangles 2-5/8" x 6-7/8"
    6 rectangles 2-5/8" x 13-1/4"
  8 strips 6-1/2" x 40" for the outer border
  8 strips 3" x 40" for the binding

• From the cocoa flannel, cut:

   2 strips 2-5/8" x 40"; from these strips, cut:

      6 rectangles 2-5/8" x 9"

• From the gold flannel, cut:

   2 strips 2-5/8" x 40"; from these strips, cut:

      6 rectangles 2-5/8" x 11-1/8"

   1 strip 11-1/2" x 40"; from this strip, cut:

      3 squares 11-1/2" x 11-1/2", cut each square
      diagonally to make 6 half-square triangles

   8 strips 6-1/2" x 40" for outer border

   8 strips 3" x 40" for binding

• From the medium blue flannel, cut:

   2 strips 2-5/8" x 40"; from these strips, cut:

      6 rectangles 2-5/8" x 11-1/8"

• From the green flannel, cut:

   1 strip 11-1/2" x 40"; from this strip, cut:

      3 squares 11-1/2" x 11-1/2", cut each square
      diagonally to make 6 half-square triangles

• From the dark green fabric, cut:

   7 strips 3-1/2" x 40" for the inner border

Assembling the Log Cabin Block

1. Sew together a navy 2-5/8" square and a bright blue 2-5/8" square to make Unit A. Press the seam toward the navy, squaring up the block if necessary. You will have 6 Unit A's.

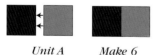

Unit A   *Make 6*

2. Sew a light blue 2-5/8" x 4-3/4" rectangle to Unit A. Press the seam toward the light blue, squaring up the block if necessary. You will have 6 Unit B's.

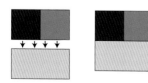

Unit B   *Make 6*

3. Sew a rust 2-5/8" x 4-3/4" rectangle to Unit B. Press the seam toward the rust, squaring up the block if necessary. You will have 6 Unit C's.

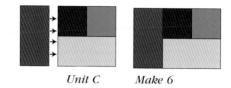

Unit C   *Make 6*

4. Sew a tan 2-5/8" x 6-7/8" rectangle to Unit C. Press the seam toward the tan, squaring up the block if necessary. You will need 6 Unit D's.

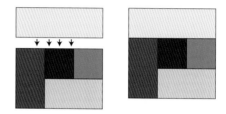

Unit D   *Make 6*

5. Sew a navy 2-5/8" x 6-7/8" rectangle to Unit D. Press seam toward the navy, squaring up the block if necessary. You will have 6 Unit E's.

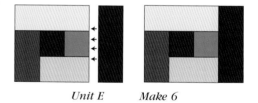

Unit E   *Make 6*

6. Sew a bright blue 2-5/8" x 9" rectangle to Unit E. Press the seam toward the bright blue, squaring up the block if necessary. You will have 6 Unit F's.

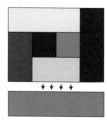

Unit F   *Make 6*

7. Sew a cocoa 2-5/8" x 9" rectangle to Unit F. Press the seam toward the cocoa, squaring up the block if necessary. You will have 6 Unit G's.

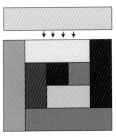 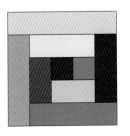

Unit G   Make 6

8. Sew a gold 2-5/8" x 11-1/8" rectangle to Unit G. Press the seam toward the gold, squaring up the block if necessary. You will have 6 Unit H's.

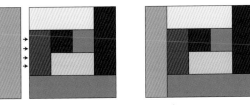

Unit H   Make 6

9. Sew a medium blue 2-5/8" x 11-1/8" rectangle to Unit H. Press the seam toward the medium blue, squaring up the block if necessary. You will have 6 Unit I's.

Unit I   Make 6

10. Sew a navy 2-5/8" x 13-1/4" rectangle to Unit I. Press seam toward the navy, squaring up the block if necessary. You will have 6 Unit J's.

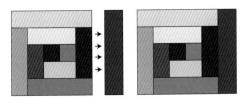

Unit J   Make 6

11. Sew a tan 2-5/8" x 13-1/4" rectangle to Unit J. Press the seam toward the tan, squaring up the block if necessary. You will have 6 Unit K's.

Unit K   Make 6

12. Sew a rust 2-5/8" x 15-3/8" rectangle to Unit K. Press seam toward the rust, squaring up the block if necessary. You will have 6 Unit L's.

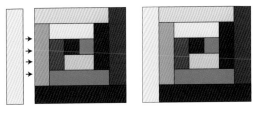
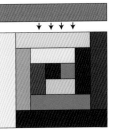 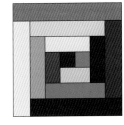

Unit L   Make 6

13. On each of the 6 blocks, sew the navy 11-1/2" triangle on the rust side of the block, and then sew the gold 11-1/2" triangle on the navy side of the block. Carefully press the seams toward the triangles.

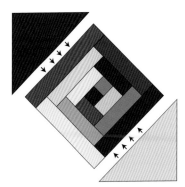

14. On each of the 6 blocks, sew the green 11-1/2" triangle on the medium blue side of the block, and then sew the rust 11-1/2" triangle on the tan side of the block. Carefully press the seams toward the triangles, squaring up the block if necessary.

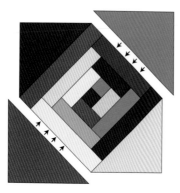

15. To complete the quilt top, sew the 6 blocks together, in three rows of two blocks. Press the seams in the direction of the least bulk.

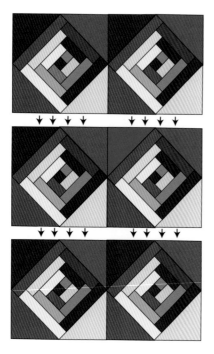

Adding the Borders

1. Measure the width of the quilt top through the center and cut 2 dark green 3-1/2" strips to that measurement. Sew these strips to the top and bottom edges of the quilt top. Press the seams toward the border.

2. Measure the length of the quilt top through the center and cut 2 dark green 3-1/2" strips to that measurement. Sew these strips to the side edges of the quilt top. Press the seams toward the border.

3. Measure the new width of the quilt top through the center and cut 2 gold 6-1/2" strips to that measurement. Sew these strips to the top and bottom edges of the inner border. Press the seams toward the border.

4. Measure the new length of the quilt top through the center and cut 2 gold 6-1/2" strips to that measurement. Sew these strips to the side edges of the inner border. Press the seams toward the border.

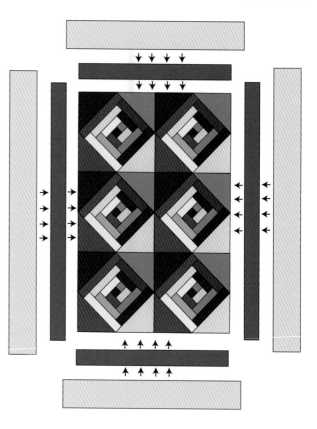

Finishing the Log Cabin Snuggler

1. Layer the quilt backing fabric, the batting, and the completed quilt top and baste the layers together.

2. Hand- or machine-stitch the quilt as desired.

3. Finish the quilt by sewing on the binding.

Log Cabin Snuggler

MAPLE LEAF

Shades of autumn are reminders
of fall's first frost with the classic
Maple Leaf block as the background
for a scene featuring a family of deer
and a scattering of falling leaves to
appliqué on a wildlife wallhanging.

Materials

Finished size is approximately 21" x 21"

Fabrics are based on 42"-wide cotton fabric that has not been washed.

7/8 yard of pale yellow fabric for background

1/4 yard of salmon fabric for background

1/4 yard of burnt orange fabric for background

1/4 yard of golden brown fabric for background

1/4 yard of brown fabric for background

1/4 yard of green fabric for background

1/4 yard of dark green fabric for pine trees and maple leaves

Scraps of light and medium green fabric for maple leaves

Scrap of rust fabric for maple leaves

Scrap of light brown fabric for fawn and antlers

Scrap of medium brown fabric for doe and tree trunks

Scrap of dark brown fabric for buck

Scrap of blue fabric for water

1 yard of fusible web

Stabilizer for appliqués

Sulky® threads to match appliqué fabrics

Maple Leaf Block

Cutting Instructions

(A 1/4" seam allowance is included in these measurements.)

• From the pale yellow fabric, cut:

1 strip 5-1/2" x 42"; from this strip, cut:

2 squares 5-1/2" x 5-1/2"

1 strip 5-7/8" x 42"; from this strip, cut:

2 squares 5-7/8" x 5-7/8"; cut squares in half diagonally to make 4 half-square triangles

1 strip 11-1/2" x 42"; from this strip, cut:

2 squares 11-1/2" x 11-1/2", cut squares in half diagonally to make 4 half-square triangles

• From the salmon fabric, cut:

1 strip 5-1/2" x 42"; from this strip, cut:

1 square 5-1/2" x 5-1/2"

• From the burnt orange fabric, cut:

1 strip 5-1/2" x 42"; from this strip, cut:

1 square 5-1/2" x 5-1/2"

• From the golden brown fabric, cut:

1 strip 5-1/2" x 42"; from this strip, cut:

1 square 5-1/2" x 5-1/2"

• From the brown fabric, cut:

1 strip 5-7/8" x 42"; from this strip, cut:

2 squares 5-7/8" x 5-7/8"; cut squares in half diagonally to make 4 half-square triangles

• From the green fabric, cut:

1 strip 4-1/2" x 42"; from this strip, cut:

4 squares 4-1/2" x 4-1/2"

1 rectangle 1-1/4" x 8" for stem on maple leaf

Assembling the Block

1. Sew 4 pale yellow 5-7/8" triangles and 4 brown 5-7/8" triangles together. Press toward the brown. You will have 4 Unit A's.

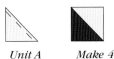

Unit A   *Make 4*

2. Sew 2 Unit A's and a 5-1/2" pale yellow square together, as shown. Press in the direction of least amount of bulk. This will be Row 1.

Row 1

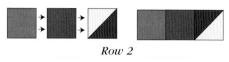

3. Sew the golden brown and the burnt orange 5-1/2" square and a Unit A together. Press in the direction of least amount of bulk. This will be Row 2.

Row 2

4. Appliqué the green stem to the 5 1/2" pale yellow square. Following manufacturer's instructions, fuse web to the wrong side of the green 1-1/4" x 8" rectangle. Trim rectangle to 3/4" wide. Fuse the stem on the diagonal center of the 5-1/2" pale yellow square. Machine stitch using a small zigzag down each long edge of the stem. Trim stem off at each corner.

5. Sew the appliquéd pale yellow 5-1/2" square, the salmon 5-1/2" square and a Unit A together, as shown. Press in the direction of least amount of bulk. This will be Row 3.

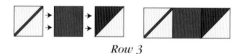

Row 3

6. Sew Row 1, Row 2, and Row 3 together, as shown. Press in the direction of least amount of bulk.

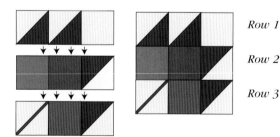

Row 1

Row 2

Row 3

7. Sew two pale yellow 11-1/2" triangles on opposite sides of the block. Press carefully toward the triangle.

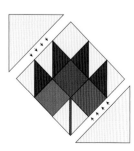

8. Sew the two remaining pale yellow 11-1/2" triangles on the remaining sides of the block, as shown. Press carefully toward the triangles. Square up the block, if necessary. Make sure to leave a 1/4" seam allowance past the intersections and make sure the corners are at 90° angles.

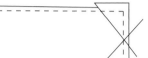

1/4" seam allowance past intersection

9. Draw a diagonal line on the wrong side of the green 4-1/2" squares, as shown.

10. Sew the 4-1/2" green squares on each pale yellow triangle on the marked diagonal line, as shown. Press the green triangle toward the outside. Trim away the middle triangle only.

Adding the Appliqués

1. Trace all appliqué templates from pages 83-85 and cut out.

2. Refer to General Instructions to prepare pieces for appliqué.

3. Use lightweight tear-away stabilizer to machine-appliqué the pieces. Place the stabilizer beneath

the fabric layers and use a small zigzag stitch to sew around each shape, smoothly covering the raw fabric edge. If your machine has stitch options, use them to detail the appliqués. After the stitching is complete, remove the stabilizer according to the manufacturer's instructions.

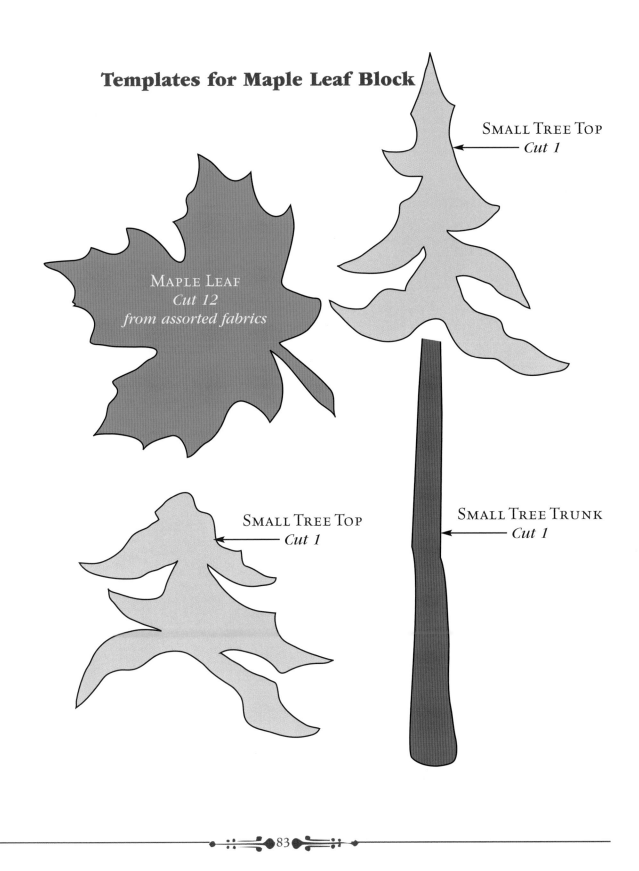

Templates for Maple Leaf Block

SMALL TREE TOP
Cut 1

MAPLE LEAF
*Cut 12
from assorted fabrics*

SMALL TREE TOP
Cut 1

SMALL TREE TRUNK
Cut 1

Templates for Maple Leaf Block

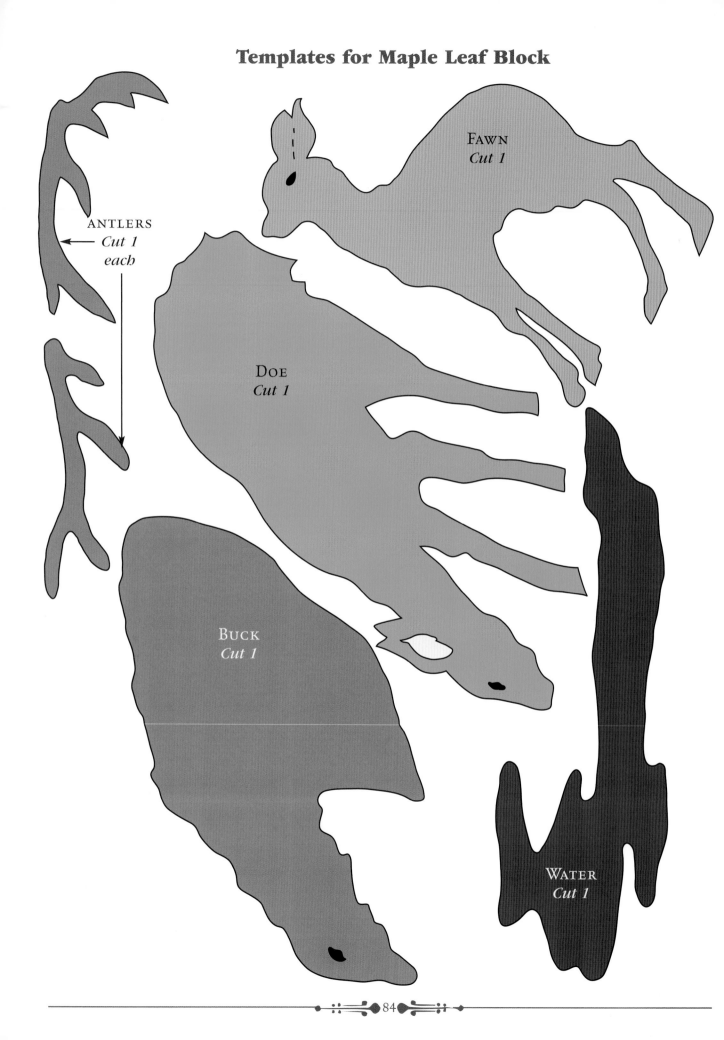

ANTLERS
*Cut 1
each*

FAWN
Cut 1

DOE
Cut 1

BUCK
Cut 1

WATER
Cut 1

Templates for Maple Leaf Block

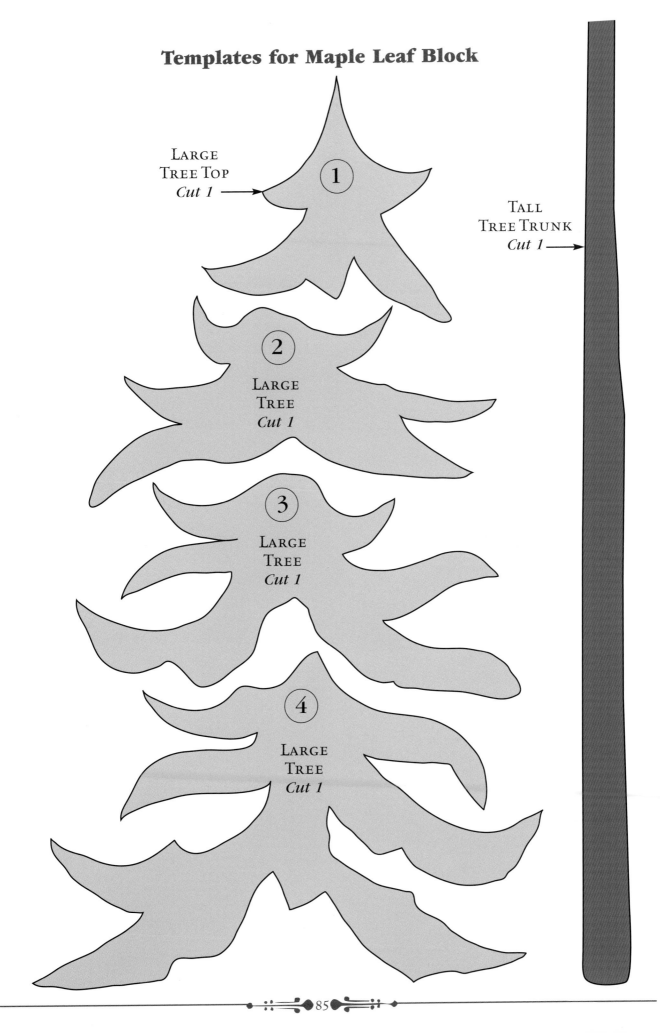

Large
Tree Top
Cut 1 →

①

② Large
Tree
Cut 1

③ Large
Tree
Cut 1

④ Large
Tree
Cut 1

Tall
Tree Trunk
Cut 1 →

Quilt it Quick

Maple Leaf Wallhanging

Materials

Finished size is approximately 33" x 33"

Fabrics are based on 42"-wide cotton fabric that has not been washed.

1 completed Maple Leaf block

■

1/4 yard of dark brown fabric for cornerstones

■

1/4 yard of burnt orange fabric for sashing

■

1 yard of dark green fabric
for borders and binding

■

43" x 43" piece of batting

■

43" x 43" piece of fabric for backing

Cutting Instructions

• From the dark brown fabric, cut:
  1 strip 2-1/2" x 42"; from this strip, cut:
    4 squares 2-1/2" x 2-1/2"

• From the burnt orange fabric cut:
  2 strips 2-1/2" x 42"; from these strips, cut:
    4 rectangles 2-1/2" x 21-1/2"

• From dark green fabric, cut:
  4 strips 4-1/2" x 42"
  5 strips 2-1/2" x 42"

Assembling the Wallhanging

1. Sew a dark brown 2-1/2" x 2-1/2" square on each end of 2 burnt orange 2-1/2" x 21-1/2" rectangles. Press toward the dark brown. You will have two Unit A's.

2. Sew a burnt orange 2-1/2" x 21-1/2" rectangle on each side of the block. Press toward the block. You will have one Unit B.

3. Sew Unit A to the top and bottom of Unit B. Press in the direction of least amount of bulk.

4. Measure the width of the wallhanging through the center to get top and bottom border measurement. Cut two strips to that length from the dark green 4-1/2"-wide strips. Sew strips to the top and bottom. Press toward the border.

5. Measure the length of the wallhanging through the center to get side border measurement. Cut two dark green strips to that length from the 4-1/2"-swide strips. Sew to each side. Press toward the border.

Finishing the Wallhanging

1. Layer the wallhanging backing fabric, batting, and quilt top.

2. Hand- or machine-quilt as desired.

3. Finish the wallhanging by sewing on the binding.

HORIZON

Sky meets water in a block with patterns

for an appliqué scene that captures

the essence of every fisherman's dream—

taking the day off with nothing

to do but fish!

Materials

Finished size is approximately 21" x 21"

Fabrics are based on 42"-wide cotton fabric that has not been washed.

3/8 yard of light blue fabric for background

1/2 yard of dark blue fabric for background

1/4 yard of light green fabric for line of trees

Scraps of medium blue and aqua fabric for water ripples

Scrap of brown fabric for canoe ribs, eagle and man's hair and pants

Scrap of dark red fabric for canoe

Scrap of golden brown fabric for inside canoe and handle on net

Scrap of light brown fabric for paddle and man's belt

Scrap of tan fabric for fishing net and eagle's head

Scrap of off-white fabric for eagle's head and man's face and arm

Scrap of green fabric for man's sleeve and fish

1 yard of fusible web

Stabilizer for appliqués

Sulky® threads to match appliqué fabrics

Horizon Block

Cutting Instructions

(A 1/4" seam allowance is included in these measurements.)

- From the light blue fabric, cut:
  1 strip 10" x 42"; from this strip, cut:
     1 rectangle 10" x 21-1/2"

- From the dark blue fabric, cut:
  1 strip 12" x 42"; from this strip, cut:
     1 rectangle 12" x 21-1/2"

Assembling the Block

1. Sew the light blue 10" x 21-1/2" rectangle to the dark blue 12" x 21-1/2" rectangle.

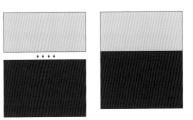

2. Press toward the dark blue.

Adding the Appliqués

1. Trace all appliqué templates from pages 92-95 and cut out.

2. Refer to General Instructions to prepare pieces for appliqué.

3. Use lightweight tear-away stabilizer to machine-appliqué the pieces. Place the stabilizer beneath the fabric layers and use a small zigzag stitch to sew around each shape, smoothly covering the raw fabric edge. If your machine has stitch options, use them to detail the appliqués. After the stitching is complete, remove the stabilizer according to the manufacturer's instructions.

TREES
Cut 1

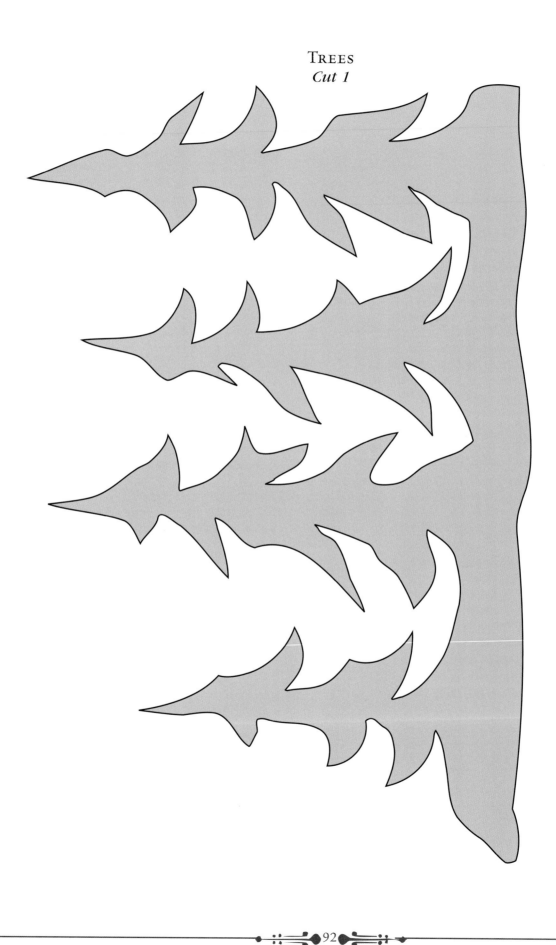

Templates for Horizon Block

Templates for Horizon Block

TREES
Cut 1

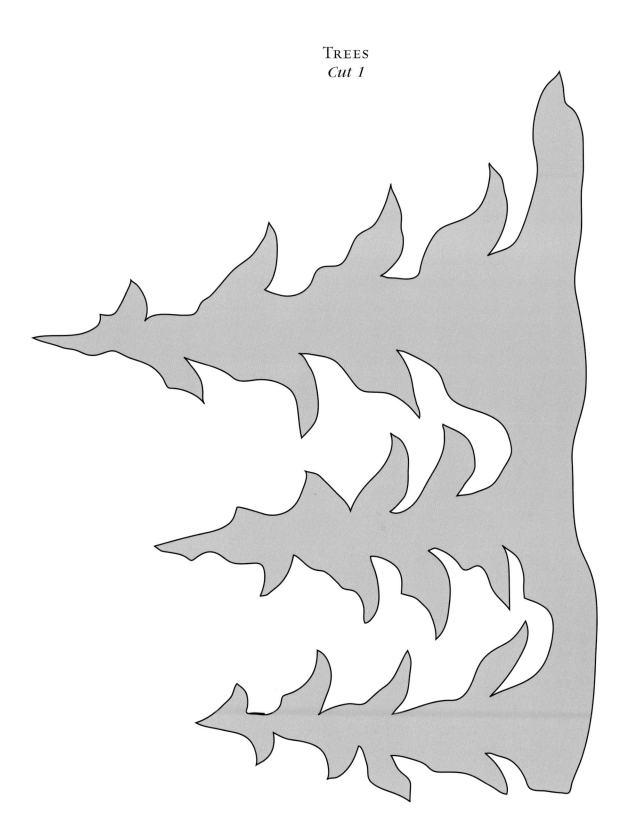

Templates for Horizon Block

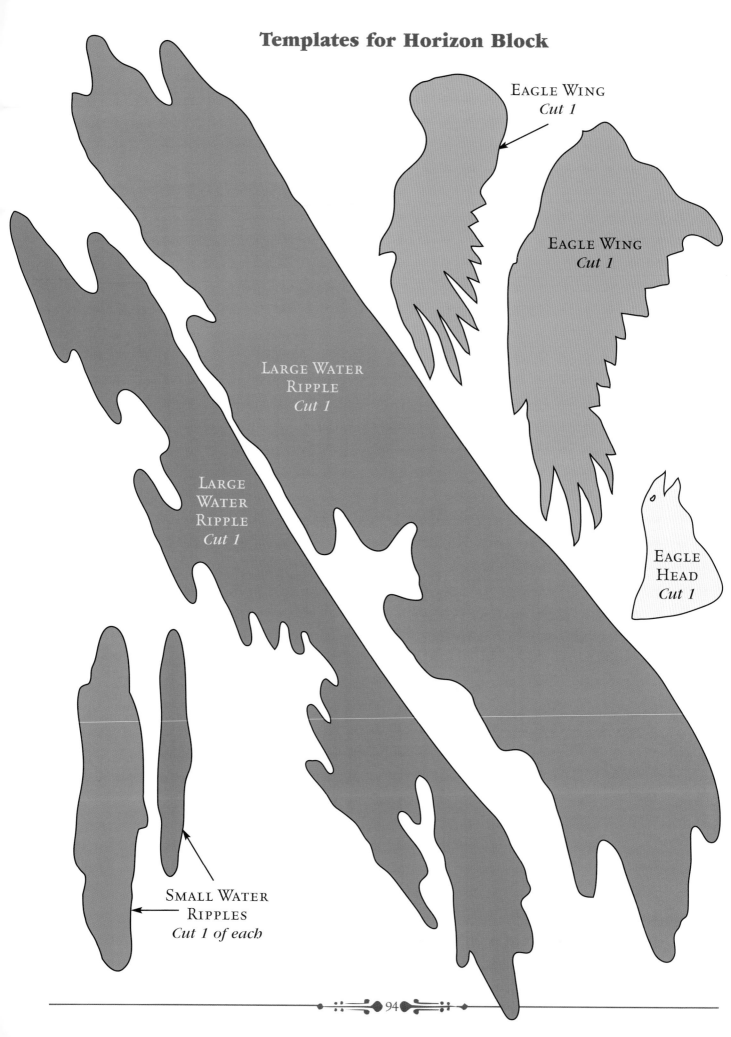

EAGLE WING
Cut 1

EAGLE WING
Cut 1

LARGE WATER RIPPLE
Cut 1

LARGE WATER RIPPLE
Cut 1

EAGLE HEAD
Cut 1

SMALL WATER RIPPLES
Cut 1 of each

Templates for Horizon Block

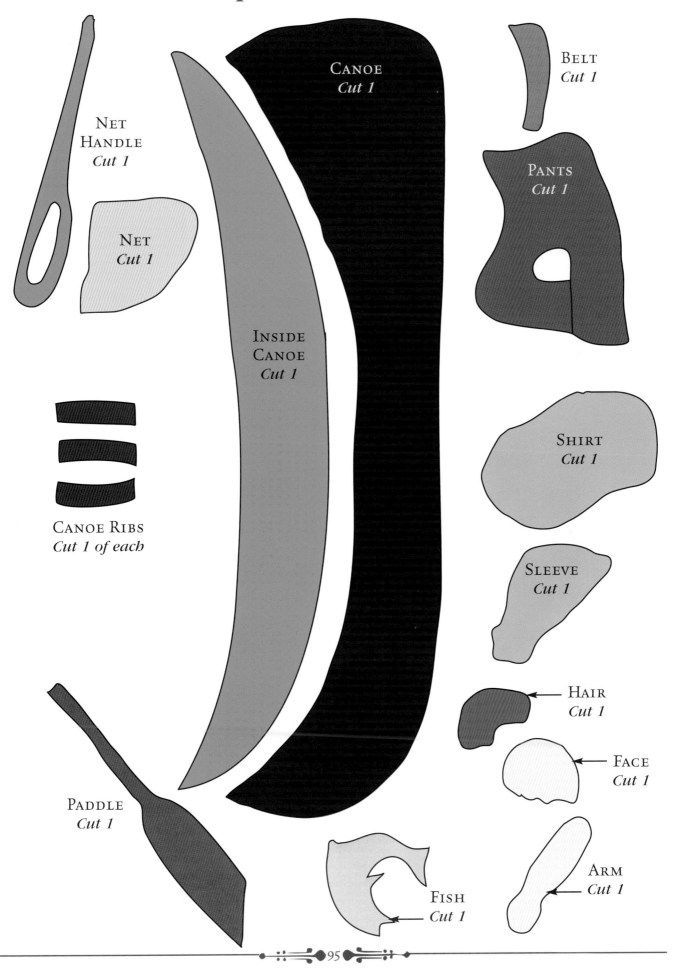

NET
HANDLE
Cut 1

NET
Cut 1

CANOE
Cut 1

BELT
Cut 1

PANTS
Cut 1

INSIDE
CANOE
Cut 1

CANOE RIBS
Cut 1 of each

SHIRT
Cut 1

SLEEVE
Cut 1

HAIR
Cut 1

FACE
Cut 1

PADDLE
Cut 1

FISH
Cut 1

ARM
Cut 1

BUTTERFLY

The old-fashioned Butterfly block
brings the meadow to life with patterns
for colorful blooms, butterflies,
and a hummingbird to appliqué
on a wildflower wallhanging
and large and small pillows.

Materials

Finished size is approximately 21" x 21"

Fabrics are based on 42"-wide cotton fabric that has not been washed.

1/2 yard of pale yellow fabric for background

1/3 yard of golden brown fabric for background

1/3 yard total of 3 assorted green fabrics for leaves, stems and hummingbird

Scrap of purple fabric for wildflowers

Scrap of periwinkle fabric for tree blossoms

Scraps of yellow, orange, gold and black fabric for butterflies and hummingbird's beak

Scrap of red fabric for hummingbird's head

Scrap of brown fabric for branch

1-1/2 yards of fusible web

Stabilizer for appliqués

Sulky® threads to match appliqué fabrics

Butterfly Block

Cutting Instructions

(A 1/4" seam allowance is included in these measurements.)

- From the pale yellow fabric, cut:
  1 strip 5-3/4" x 42"; from this strip, cut:
      4 squares 5-3/4" x 5-3/4"
  1 strip 6-1/8" x 42"; from this strip, cut:
      6 squares 6-1/8" x 6-1/8"; cut squares in half
      diagonally to make 12 half-square triangles

- From the golden brown fabric, cut:
  1 strip 6-1/8" x 42"; from this strip, cut
      6 squares 6-1/8" x 6-1/8"; cut squares in half
      diagonally to make 12 half-square triangles

Assembling the Block

1. Sew the pale yellow 6-1/8" half-square triangles and the golden brown 6-1/8" half-square triangles together. Press toward the golden brown. You will need 12 Unit A's.

Unit A   *Make 12*

2. Sew 2 Unit A's together. Press in the direction of least amount of bulk. You will have 4 Unit B's.

Unit B   *Make 4*

3. Sew 2 Unit A's together. Press in the direction of least amount of bulk. You will have 2 Unit C's.

Unit C   *Make 2*

4. Sew a pale yellow 5-3/4" square on each end of a Unit C, as shown. Press toward the square. You will have 2 Unit D's.

Unit D   *Make 2*

5. Sew 4 Unit B's together, as shown. Press in the direction of least amount of bulk. You will have 1 Unit E.

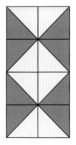
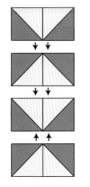

Unit E   *Make 1*

Butterfly Block

6. Sew a Unit D to each side of Unit E. Press in the direction of least amount of bulk.

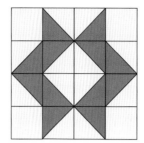

Adding the Appliqués

1. Trace all appliqué templates from pages 100-103 and cut out.

2. Refer to General Instructions to prepare pieces for appliqué.

3. Use lightweight tear-away stabilizer to machine-appliqué the pieces. Place the stabilizer beneath the fabric layers and use a small zigzag stitch to sew around each shape, smoothly covering the raw fabric edge. If your machine has stitch options, use them to detail the appliqués. After the stitching is complete, remove the stabilizer according to the manufacturer's instructions.

Templates for Butterfly Block

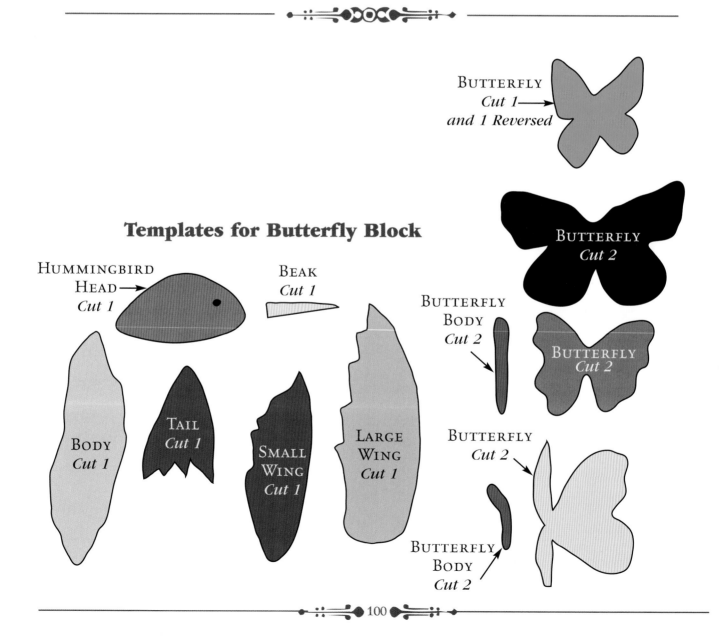

BUTTERFLY
Cut 1—
and 1 Reversed

BUTTERFLY
Cut 2

HUMMINGBIRD
HEAD
Cut 1

BEAK
Cut 1

BUTTERFLY
BODY
Cut 2

BUTTERFLY
Cut 2

BODY
Cut 1

TAIL
Cut 1

SMALL
WING
Cut 1

LARGE
WING
Cut 1

BUTTERFLY
Cut 2

BUTTERFLY
BODY
Cut 2

100

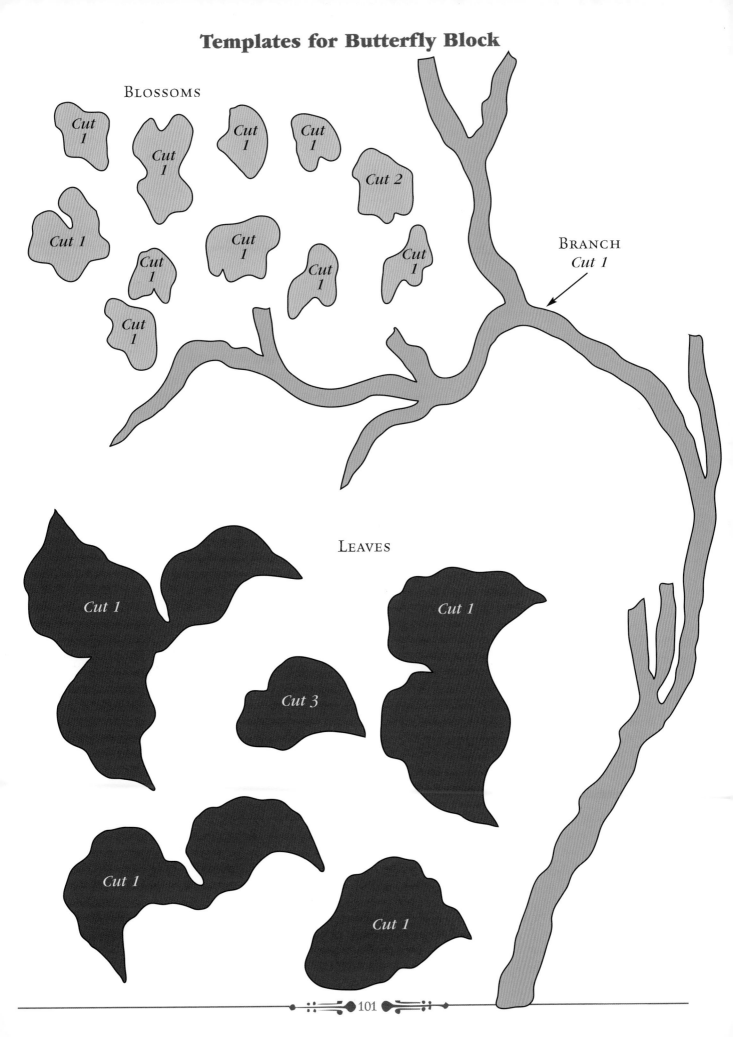

Templates for Butterfly Block

BLOSSOMS

Cut 1

Cut 1

Cut 1

Cut 1

Cut 2

Cut 1

Cut 1

Cut 1

Cut 1

Cut 1

Cut 1

Cut 1

BRANCH
Cut 1

LEAVES

Cut 1

Cut 1

Cut 3

Cut 1

Cut 1

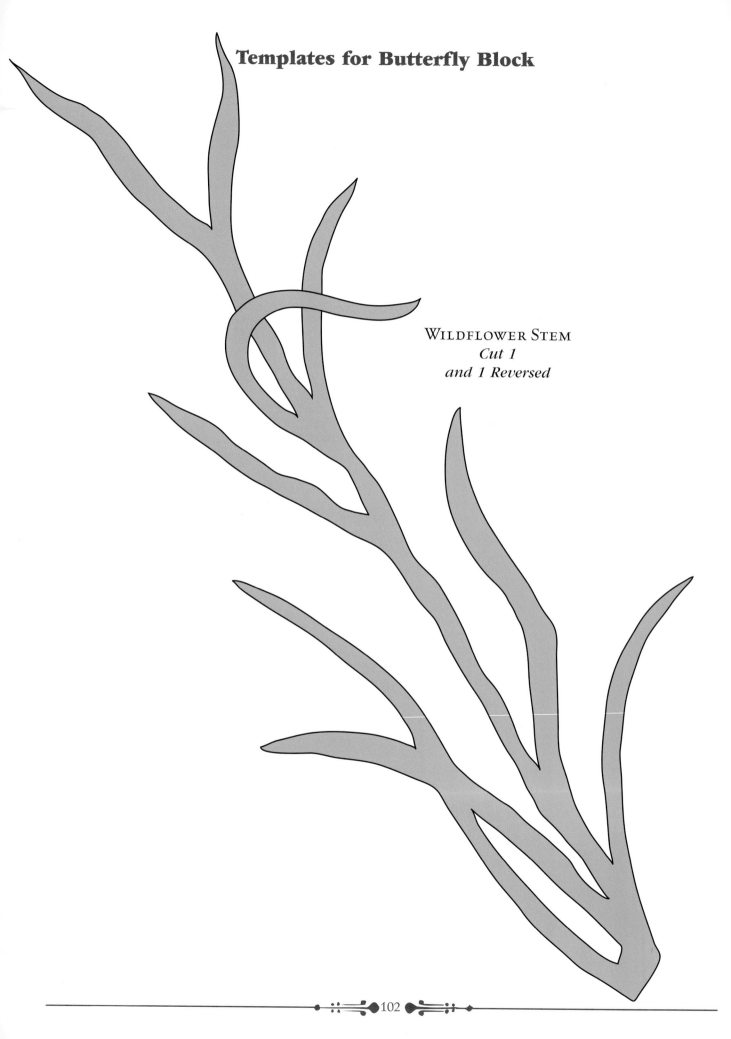

Templates for Butterfly Block

WILDFLOWER STEM
*Cut 1
and 1 Reversed*

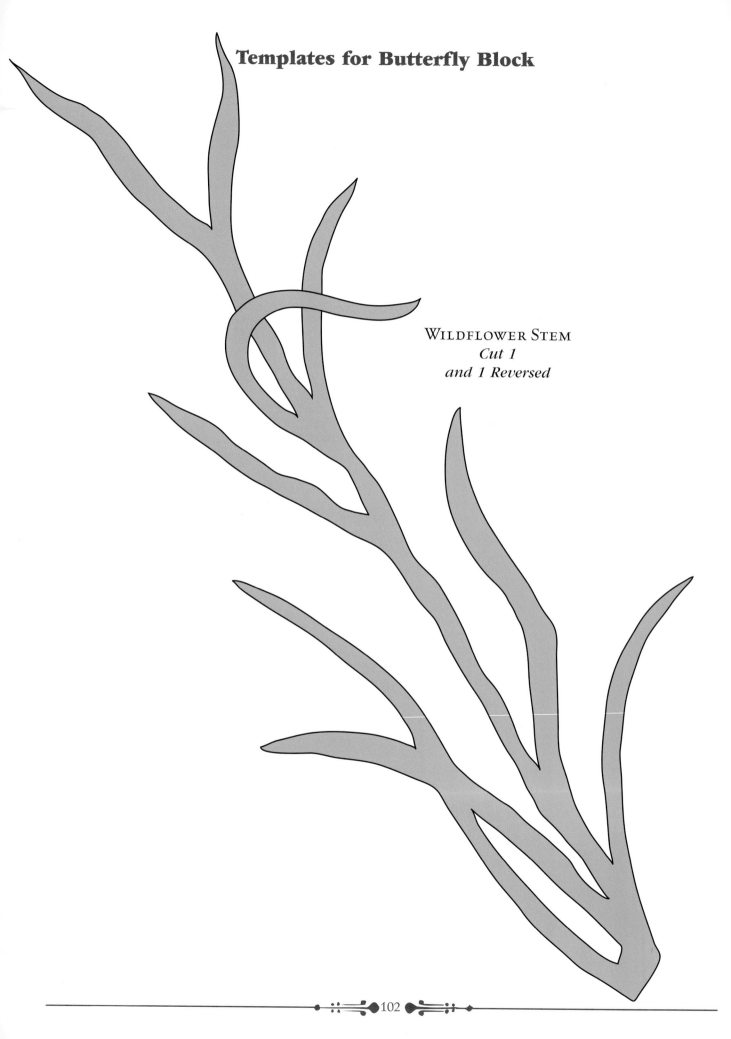

Templates for Butterfly Block

Templates for Butterfly Block

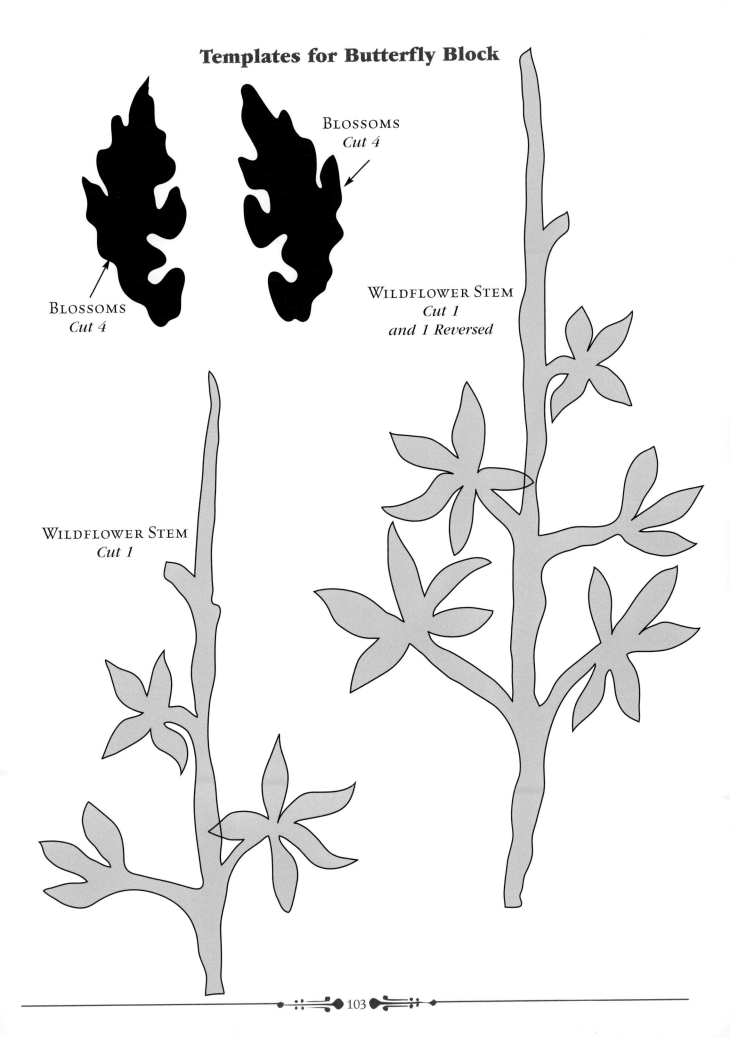

BLOSSOMS
Cut 4

BLOSSOMS
Cut 4

WILDFLOWER STEM
*Cut 1
and 1 Reversed*

WILDFLOWER STEM
Cut 1

Quilt it Quick
Butterfly Wallhanging

Materials

Finished size is approximately 33" x 33"

Fabrics are based on 42"-wide cotton fabric that has not been washed.

One completed Butterfly Block

Scraps of dark green fabric for cornerstones

1/3 yard of purple fabric for sashing

1 yard of pale yellow fabric for borders and binding

43" x 43" piece of batting

43" x 43" piece of fabric for backing

Cutting Instructions

• From the dark green fabric, cut:
  4 squares 2-1/2" x 2-1/2" for cornerstones

• From the purple fabric, cut:
  4 strips 2-1/2" x 42"; from these strips, cut:
    4 rectangles 2-1/2" x 21-1/2" for sashing

• From the pale yellow fabric, cut:
  4 strips 4-1/2" x 42" for border
  5 strips 2-1/2" x 42" for binding

Assembling the Wallhanging

1. Sew a dark green 2-1/2" x 2-1/2" square on each end of 2 purple 2-1/2" x 21-1/2" rectangles. Press toward the dark green. You will have two Unit A's.

2. Sew a purple 2-1/2" x 21-1/2" rectangle on each side of the block. You will have one Unit B.

3. Sew Unit A to the top and bottom of Unit B. Press in the direction of least amount of bulk.

4. Measure the width of the wallhanging through the center to get top and bottom border measurement. Cut two strips that length from the purple 4-1/2"- wide strips. Sew strips to the top and bottom. Press toward the border.

5. Measure the length of the wallhanging through the center to get side border measurement. Cut two pale yellow strips that length from the 4-1/2" wide strips. Sew strips to each side. Press toward the border.

Finishing the Wallhanging

1. Layer the backing fabric, batting, and top.

2. Hand- or machine-quilt as desired.

3. Finish the wallhanging by sewing on the binding.

Quilt it Quick

Butterfly Pillows

Materials

Finished size is approximately 17" x 17" for large pillow and 10" x 10" for small pillow

1 yard of cream fabric for pillow backgrounds; outer border and backing of large pillow

1/4 yard of purple fabric for inner border of large pillow

1/3 yard of teal fabric for borders and back of small pillow

16" x 16" pillow form for large pillow and fiberfill for small pillow

Scraps of light green, black, yellow, red, dark and light purple fabric for flower stems, butterfly bodies, hummingbird, and wildflowers

1/2 yard of fusible webbing

12" x 12" piece of batting for large pillow

Sulky® threads to match appliqué fabrics

Butterfly Pillow

Cutting Instructions

• From the cream fabric, cut:
  10" x 10" square for background
  2 strips 3" x 42" for outer border

• From the purple fabric, cut:
  2 strips 2" x 42"; from these strips, cut:
    2 strips 2" x 10" for inner border

Adding the Appliqués

1. Trace appliqué templates from pages 100-103; cut out.

2. Refer to General Instructions to prepare pieces for appliqué.

3. Use lightweight tear-away stabilizer to machine-appliqué the pieces. Place the stabilizer beneath the fabric layers and use a small zigzag stitch to sew around each shape, smoothly covering the raw fabric edge. If your machine has stitch options, use them to detail the appliqués. After the stitching is complete, remove the stabilizer according to the manufacturer's instructions.

Assembling the Pillow

1. Sew a 2" x 10" purple strip to the top and bottom of pillow center. Press toward the outside. Measure sides of pillow and cut 2 strips of purple fabric to that measurement, and sew to sides.

2. Measure the width of the pillow top through the center. Cut 2 strips of 3"-wide cream fabric to that measurement, and sew to top and bottom. Press toward the outside. Measure pillow through the center lengthwise. Cut 2 strips to that measurement and sew to the sides of the pillow.

3. To machine quilt the pillow top, layer batting and pillow top. Quilt as desired.

4. Press and trim excess batting from the pillow top. Layer pillow backing right side up and pillow top wrong side up. Stitch 1/4" seam around pillow top, leaving an opening at bottom to insert pillow form or stuffing. Clip corners and any excess backing fabric. Turn. Insert pillow form and stitch opening closed.

Hummingbird Pillow

Cutting Instructions

• From the cream fabric, cut:
  6-1/2" x 6-1/2" square

• From the teal fabric, cut:
  1 strip 2-1/2" x 42" for border
    2 rectangles 2-1/2" x 6-1/2"
    2 rectangles 2-1/2" x 10-1/2"

Assembling the Pillow

Refer to steps 2–4 for the Butterfly Pillow, eliminating sashing and quilting.

DELECTABLE MOUNTAIN

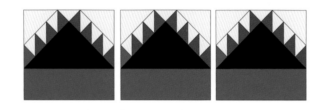

Standing the test of time,

the Delectable Mountain block rises

majestically in an 8-block snuggler

and as the background of an appliqué

scene featuring the Granola Girl®

on a hike for a better view.

DELECTABLE MOUNTAIN BLOCK

Materials

Finished size is approximately 21" x 21"

Fabrics are based on 42"-wide cotton fabric that has not been washed.

1/2 yard of tan fabric for background

■

1/2 yard of teal fabric for background

■

2/3 yard of dark purple fabric for background

■

1/4 yard total of medium green fabric for trees

■

1/8 yard of light brown fabric for tree trunks and antlers

■

1/4 yard of dark brown fabric for hiking path

■

Scraps of pale blue fabric for clouds

■

Scraps of fabric for moose, girl's hair, face, hand, legs, walking stick, sweatshirt, shorts and boots

■

3/4 yard of fusible web

■

Stabilizer for appliqués

■

Sulky® threads to match appliqué fabrics

Delectable Mountain Block

Cutting Instructions

(A 1/4" seam allowance is included in these measurements.)

• From the tan fabric, cut:
  1 strip 4-5/8" x 42"; from this strip, cut:
      4 squares 4-5/8" x 4-5/8"; cut squares in half diagonally to make 8 half-square triangles
      Note: 1 triangle will not be used.
  1 strip 8-5/8" x 42"; from this strip, cut:
      1 square 8-5/8" x 8-5/8"; cut square in half diagonally to make 2 half-square triangles

• From the teal fabric, cut:
  1 strip 8-1/2" x 42"; from this strip, cut:
      1 rectangle 8-1/2" x 21-1/2"
  1 strip 4-5/8" x 42"; from this strip, cut:
      4 squares 4-5/8" x 4-5/8"; cut squares in half diagonally to make 8 triangles

• From the dark purple fabric, cut:
  1 strip 15-5/8" x 42"; from this strip, cut:
      1 square 15-5/8" x 15-5/8"; cut square in half diagonally to make 2 half-square triangles
  Note: 1 triangle will not be used.

Assembling the Block

1. Sew 6 tan 4-5/8" half-square triangles and 6 teal 4-5/8" half-square triangles together. Press toward the teal. You will have 6 Unit A's.

Unit A   *Make 6*

2. Sew 3 Unit A's together, exactly as shown. Press in the direction of least amount of bulk. You will have 1 Unit B.

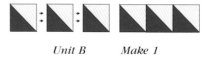

Unit B   *Make 1*

3. Sew a tan 4-5/8" half-square triangle to the left side of Unit B, exactly as shown. Press toward the tan triangle, carefully. You will have 1 Unit C.

Unit C   *Make 1*

4. Sew a teal 4-5/8" half-square triangle to the right side of Unit C, as shown. Press toward the teal triangle, carefully. You will have 1 Unit D.

Unit D   *Make 1*

5. Sew 3 Unit A's together, as shown. Press in the direction of least amount of bulk. You will have 1 Unit E.

Unit E   *Make 1*

6. Sew a teal 4-5/8" half-square triangle to the left side of Unit E, as shown. Press toward the teal triangle, carefully. You will have 1 Unit F.

Unit F   *Make 1*

7. Sew Unit F to the left side of the purple 15-5/8" half-square triangle, as shown. Press toward the purple triangle, carefully. You will have 1 Unit G.

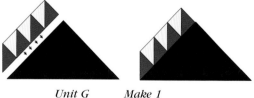

Unit G   *Make 1*

8. Sew Unit D to the right side of Unit G, as shown. Press toward the purple triangle, carefully. You will have 1 Unit H.

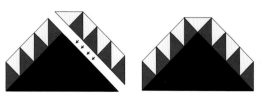

Unit H

9. Sew a tan 8-5/8" half-square triangle on each side of Unit H, as shown. Press toward the tan triangle, carefully. You will have 1 Unit I.

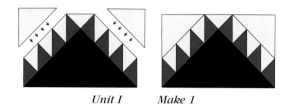

Unit I   *Make 1*

10. Sew the 8-1/2" x 21-1/2" teal rectangle to Unit I, as shown. Press toward the rectangle, carefully.

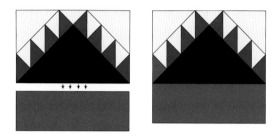

11. Square up the block, if necessary. Leave a 1/4" seam allowance past the intersection and make sure the corners are at 90° angles.

1/4" seam allowance past intersection

Adding the Appliqués

1. Trace all appliqué templates from pages 113-115 and cut out.

2. Refer to General Instructions to prepare pieces for appliqué.

3. Use lightweight tear-away stabilizer to machine-appliqué the pieces. Place the stabilizer beneath the fabric layers and use a small zigzag stitch to sew around each shape, smoothly covering the raw fabric edge. If your machine has stitch options, use them to detail the appliqués. After the stitching is complete, remove the stabilizer according to the manufacturer's instructions.

Templates for Delectable Mountain Block

TREE
Cut 1

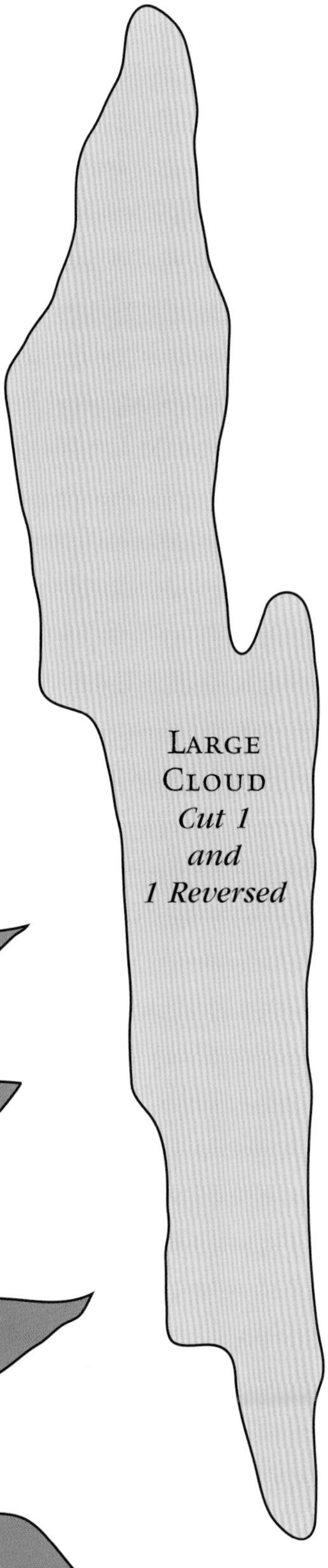

LARGE
CLOUD
*Cut 1
and
1 Reversed*

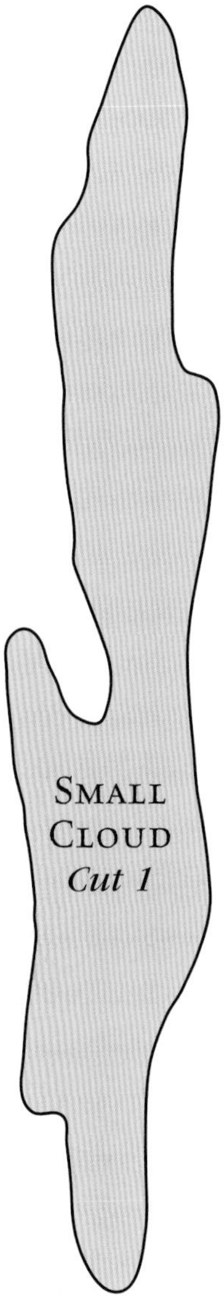

SMALL
CLOUD
Cut 1

Templates for Delectable Mountain Block

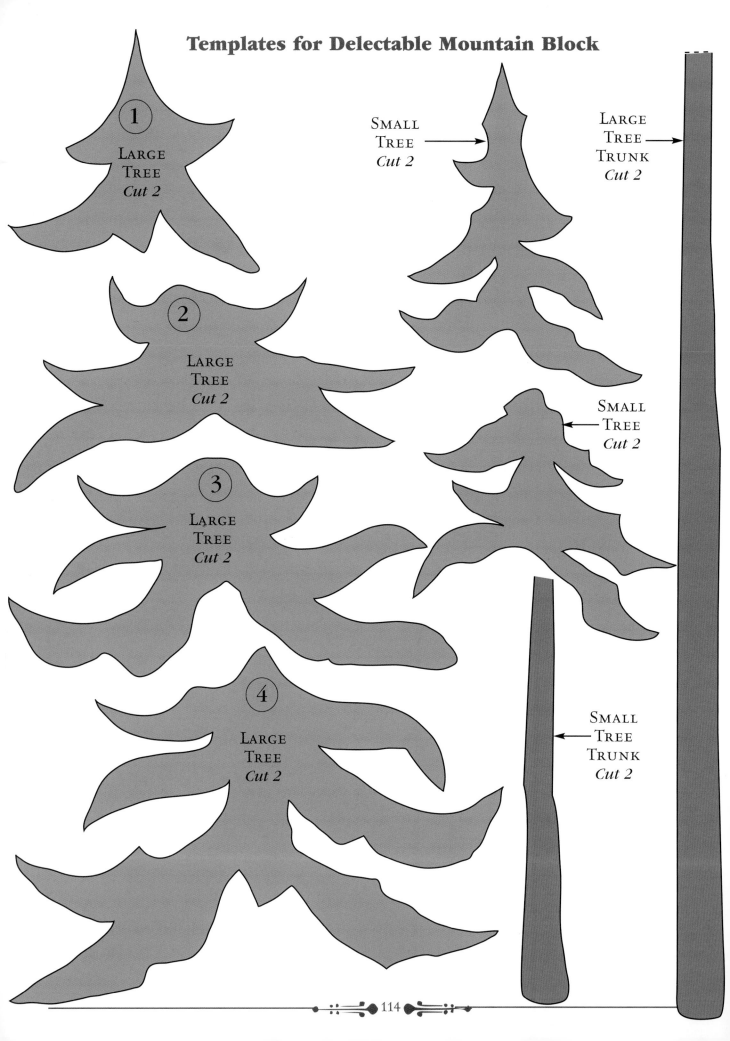

①
Large
Tree
Cut 2

②
Large
Tree
Cut 2

③
Large
Tree
Cut 2

④
Large
Tree
Cut 2

Small
Tree
Cut 2

Large
Tree
Trunk
Cut 2

Small
Tree
Cut 2

Small
Tree
Trunk
Cut 2

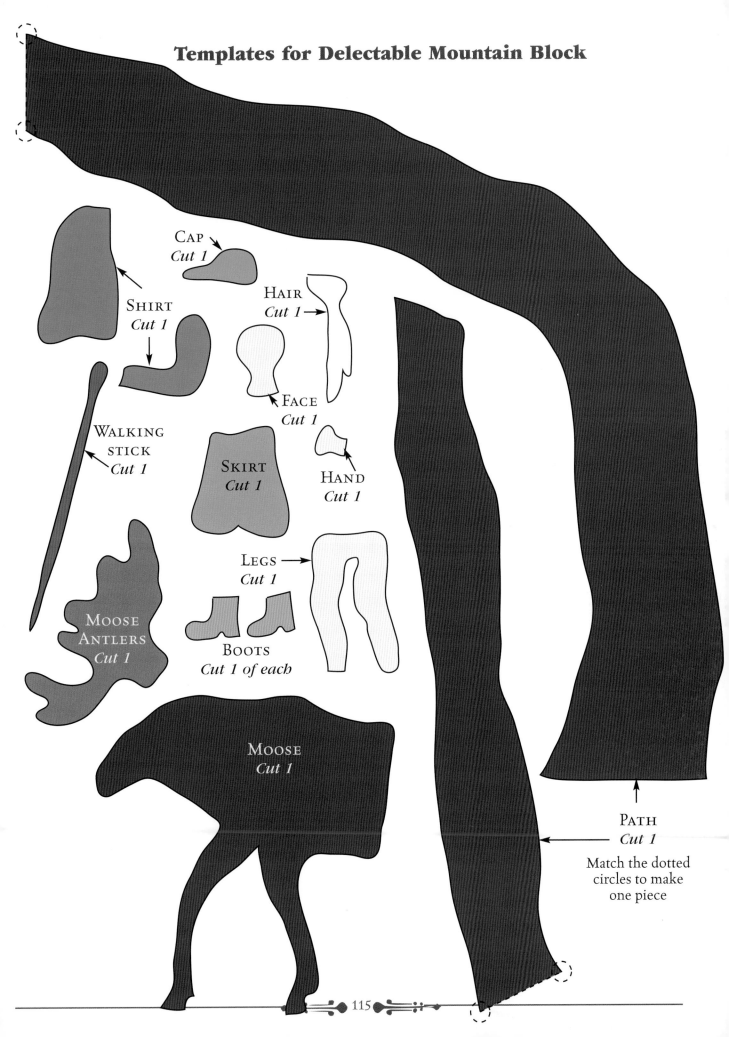

Templates for Delectable Mountain Block

CAP
Cut 1

HAIR
Cut 1

SHIRT
Cut 1

FACE
Cut 1

WALKING stick
Cut 1

SKIRT
Cut 1

HAND
Cut 1

LEGS
Cut 1

MOOSE ANTLERS
Cut 1

BOOTS
Cut 1 of each

MOOSE
Cut 1

PATH
Cut 1

Match the dotted circles to make one piece

DELECTABLE MOUNTAIN SNUGGLER

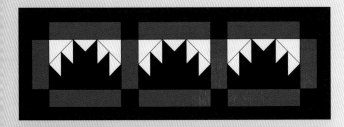

Materials

Finished size is approximately 61" x 78"

Fabrics are based on 42"-wide cotton fabric that has not been washed.

1 yard of pale lavender fabric
for blocks

■

5/8 yard of medium purple fabric
for blocks

■

1-1/4 yards of dark purple fabric for blocks,
cornerstones and inner border triangles

■

1-1/2 yards of lavender fabric for inner border

■

1-1/8 yards of light teal fabric for sashing

■

2 yards of dark teal fabric for inner border
triangles, outer border and binding

■

69" x 86" piece of batting

■

5 yards of fabric for backing

Delectable Mountain Block

Make 8 Blocks

Cutting Instructions

(A 1/4" seam allowance is included in these measurements.)

- From the pale lavender fabric, cut:
  3 strips 4-7/8" x 42"; from these strips, cut:
      20 squares 4-7/8" x 4-7/8"; cut squares
      diagonally in half to make 40 half-square triangles
  2 strips 6-5/8" x 42"; from these strips, cut:
      8 squares 6-5/8" x 6-5/8"; cut squares diagonally
      to make 16 half-square triangles

- From the medium purple fabric, cut:
  3 strips 4-7/8" x 42"; from these strips, cut:
      24 squares 4-7/8" x 4-7/8"; cut squares
      diagonally to make 48 half-square triangles

- From the dark purple fabric, cut:
  2 strips 3-1/2" x 42"; from these strips, cut:
      15 squares 3-1/2" x 3-1/2" for cornerstones
  2 strips 12-7/8" x 42"; from these strips, cut:
      4 squares 12-7/8" x 12-7/8"; cut squares
      diagonally to make 8 half-square triangles
  1 strip 6-7/8" x 42"; from this strip, cut:
      2 squares 6-7/8" x 6-7/8"; cut these squares
      diagonally to make 4 half-square triangles

- From the lavender fabric, cut:
  7 strips 6-1/2" x 42" for inner border

- From the light teal fabric, cut:
  9 strips 3-1/2" x 42"; from these strips, cut:
      10 rectangles 3-1/2" x 17-3/4"
      12 rectangles 3-1/2" x 11-3/4"

- From the dark teal fabric, cut:
  - 1 strip 6-7/8" x 42"; from these strips, cut:
    - 2 squares 6-7/8" x 6-7/8"; cut these squares diagonally to make 4 half-square triangles
  - 8 strips 3-1/2" x 42" for outer border
  - 7 strips 3" x 42" for binding

Assembling the Block

1. Sew 32 pale lavender 4-7/8" triangles and 32 medium purple 4-7/8" triangles together. Press toward the dark purple. You will have 32 Unit A's.

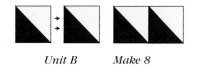

Unit A   Make 32

2. Sew 2 Unit A's together, as shown. Press in the direction of least amount of bulk. You will have 8 Unit B's.

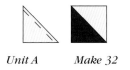

Unit B   Make 8

3. Sew a pale lavender 4-7/8" triangle to the left side of a Unit B. Press toward the pale lavender. You will have 8 Unit C's.

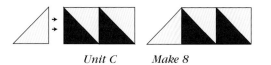

Unit C   Make 8

4. Sew a medium purple 4-7/8" triangle to the right side of a Unit C, exactly as shown. Press toward the medium purple triangle. You will have 8 Unit D's.

Unit D   Make 8

5. Sew 2 Unit A's together, exactly as shown. Press in the direction of least amount of bulk. You will have 8 Unit E's.

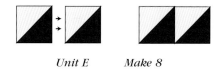

Unit E   Make 8

6. Sew a medium purple 4-7/8" triangle to the left side of a Unit E, exactly as shown. Press toward the medium purple triangle. You will have 8 Unit F's.

Unit F   Make 8

7. Sew Unit F to the left side of each of the dark purple 12-7/8" triangle, as shown. Press toward the dark. You will have 8 Unit G's.

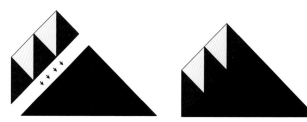

Unit G   Make 8

8. Sew Unit D to the right side of Unit G, as shown. Press toward the dark. You will have 8 Unit H's.

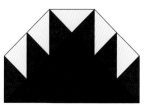

Unit H   Make 8

9. Sew a pale lavender 6-5/8" triangle on each side of Unit H, as shown. Press toward the pale lavender. You will have 8 Unit I's.

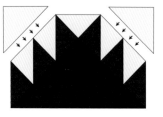 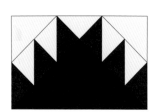

Unit I   *Make 8*

10. Square up the block, if necessary. Leave a 1/4" seam allowance past the intersection and make sure the corners are 90° angles.

Adding the Sashing

1. Sew 3 dark purple 3-1/2" squares to 2 light teal 3-1/2" x 17-3/4" rectangles, as shown. Press toward the teal. You will have 5 Unit J's.

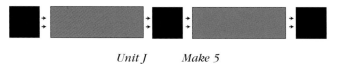

Unit J   *Make 5*

2. Sew 3 light teal 3-1/2" x 11-3/4" rectangles and 2 Unit I's together, as shown. Press toward the light teal. You will have 4 rows.

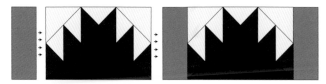

Make 4 rows

3. Sew the Unit J's and the four rows together, as shown. Press in the direction of least amount of bulk.

Adding the Borders

1. Sew the 4 dark purple 6-7/8" triangles and the 4 dark teal 6-7/8" triangles together, as shown. Press toward the dark purple. You will have 4 dark purple/dark teal squares.

2. Measure the width of the quilt top through the center to get top and bottom measurement. Cut 2 strips to that length from the lavender 6-1/2" wide strips. Set aside.

3. Measure the length of the quilt top through the center to get side measurement. Cut 2 strips that length from the lavender 6-1/2"- wide strips.

4. Sew the dark purple/dark teal squares to each end of the lavender 6-1/2"- wide side border strips, as shown. Press in the direction of least amount of bulk. Set aside.

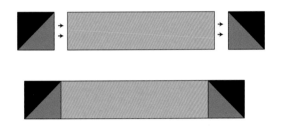

5. Sew the lavender 6-1/2"-wide inner border strips to the top and bottom of the quilt top. Press toward the dark.

6. Sew the side inner border strips from step 4 to the quilt top. Press toward the dark.

7. Measure the new width of the quilt top through the center to get top and bottom measurement. Cut 2 strips that length from the 3-1/2" dark teal strips. Sew strips to the quilt top and bottom. Press toward the dark.

8. Measure the new length of the quilt top through the center to get side border measurement. Cut 2 strips that length from the 3-1/2" dark teal strips. Sew to the sides of the quilt top. Press toward the dark.

Finishing the Quilt

1. Layer the quilt backing fabric, batting, and quilt top. Baste the layers together.

2. Hand- or machine-quilt as desired.

3. Finish the quilt by sewing on the binding.

Delectable Mountain Snuggler

TREE OF LIFE

The Tree of Life block is the inspiration
for a scattering of stars and a forest of
evergreens to appliqué on the block and a
woodland wallhanging.

Materials

Finished size is approximately 21" x 21"

Fabrics are based on 42"-wide cotton fabric that has not been washed.

1/2 yard of brown fabric for background
∎
2/3 yards of cream fabric for background
∎
1/4 yard of dark green fabric for background
∎
1/2 yard of green fabric for background
∎
Scraps of 3 assorted green fabrics for trees
∎
Scraps of gold fabric for small stars
∎
Scraps of pale yellow fabric for large stars
∎
Scrap of brown fabric for tree trunks
∎
1-1/4 yards of fusible web
∎
Stabilizer for appliqués
∎
Sulky® threads to match appliqué fabrics

Cutting Instructions

(A 1/4" seam allowance is included in these measurements.)

• From the cream fabric, cut:
  1 strip 3-7/8" x 42"; from this strip, cut:
    7 squares 3-7/8" x 3-7/8"; cut these squares in half diagonally to make 14 half-square triangles
  1 strip 3-1/2" x 42"; from this strip, cut:
    2 squares 3-1/2" x 3-1/2"
  1 strip 9-7/8" x 42"; from this strip, cut:
    1 square 9-7/8" x 9-7/8"; cut square in half diagonally to make 2 half-square triangles
    Note: 1 triangle will not be used.

• From the dark green fabric, cut:
  1 strip 3-7/8" x 42"; from this strip, cut:
    7 squares 3-7/8" x 3-7/8"; cut squares in half diagonally to make 14 half-square triangles

• From the green fabric, cut:
  1 strip 9-7/8" x 42"; from this strip, cut:
    1 square 9-7/8" x 9-7/8"; cut square in half diagonally to make half-square triangles
    Note: 1 triangle will not be used.

• From the brown fabric, cut:
  1 strip 11-1/2" x 42"; from this strip cut:
    2 squares 11-1/2" x 11-1/2" ; cut squares in half diagonally to make 4 half-square triangles
  1 rectangle 3/4" x 8 1/2" for tree trunk

Assembling the Block

1. Sew the cream 3-7/8" half-square triangles and the dark green 3-7/8" half-square triangles together. Press toward the dark green. You will have 14 Unit A's.

Unit A   Make 14

2. Appliqué the brown tree trunk to the cream 9-7/8" half-square triangle. Following manufacturer's instructions, fuse web to the wrong side of the 3/4" x 8-1/2" brown rectangle. Trim the rectangle to 5/8" wide. Position the trunk in the middle of the 9-7/8" half- square triangle and fuse. Machine stitch using a small zigzag down each long edge of the trunk. Trim trunk off at each raw edge.

3. Sew the appliquéd triangle and the green 9-7/8" half-square triangle together, as shown. Press toward the dark green. You will have 1 Unit B.

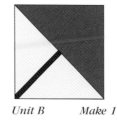

Unit B   Make 1

4. Sew 3 Unit A's together, exactly as shown. Press in the direction of least amount of bulk. You will have 1 Unit C.

Unit C   Make 1

5. Sew 3 Unit A's together, as shown. Press in direction of least amount of bulk. You will have 1 Unit D.

Unit D   Make 1

6. Sew a cream 3-1/2" square to the left side of Unit C, exactly as shown. Press in the direction of least amount of bulk. You will have 1 Unit E.

Unit E   Make 1

7. Sew Unit D to the left side of Unit B, as shown. Press toward Unit B. You will have 1 Unit F.

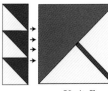

Unit F   Make 1

8. Sew Unit E to the right side of Unit F, as shown. Press toward the large triangle. You will have 1 Unit G.

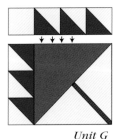

Unit G   Make 1

9. Sew 4 Unit A's together, as shown. Press in direction of least amount of bulk. You will have 1 Unit H.

Unit H

10. Sew 4 Unit A's together, as shown. Press in the direction of least amount of bulk. You will have 1 Unit I.

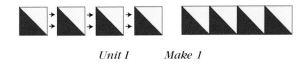

Unit I   Make 1

11. Sew a cream 3-1/2" square to the left side of Unit I, as shown. Press in the direction of least amount of bulk. You will have 1 Unit J.

Unit J   Make 1

12. Sew Unit H to the left side of Unit G, as shown. Press in the direction of least amount of bulk. You will have 1 Unit K.

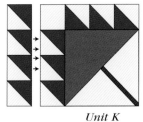

Unit K   Make 1

13. Sew Unit J to Unit K, as shown. Press in the direction of least amount of bulk.

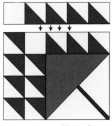

Unit L   Make 1

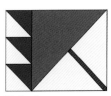

14. Sew 2 brown 11-1/2" half-square triangles on opposite sides of the Unit L block, as shown. Press carefully toward the triangles.

15. Sew the remaining 2 brown 11-1/2" half-square triangles on the opposite sides of the block, as shown. Press carefully toward the triangle. Square up the block, if necessary. Leave a 1/4" seam allowance past the intersection and make sure the corners are at 90° angles.

1/4" seam allowance past intersection

Adding the Appliqués

1. Trace all appliqué templates from pages 128-129 and cut out.

2. Refer to General Instructions to prepare pieces for appliqué.

3. Use lightweight tear-away stabilizer to machine appliqué the pieces. Place the stabilizer beneath the fabric layers and use a small zigzag stitch to sew around each shape, smoothly covering the raw fabric edge. If your machine has stitch options, use them to detail the appliqués. After the stitching is complete, remove the stabilizer according to the manufacturer's instructions.

Templates for Tree of Life Block

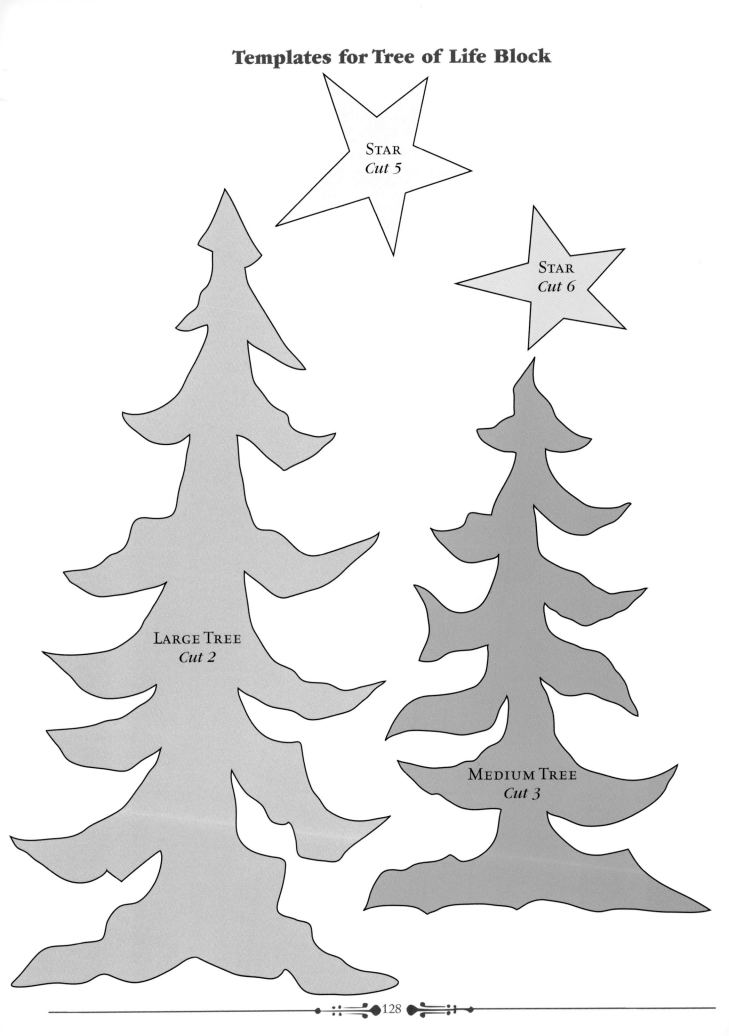

STAR
Cut 5

STAR
Cut 6

LARGE TREE
Cut 2

MEDIUM TREE
Cut 3

Templates for Tree of Life Block

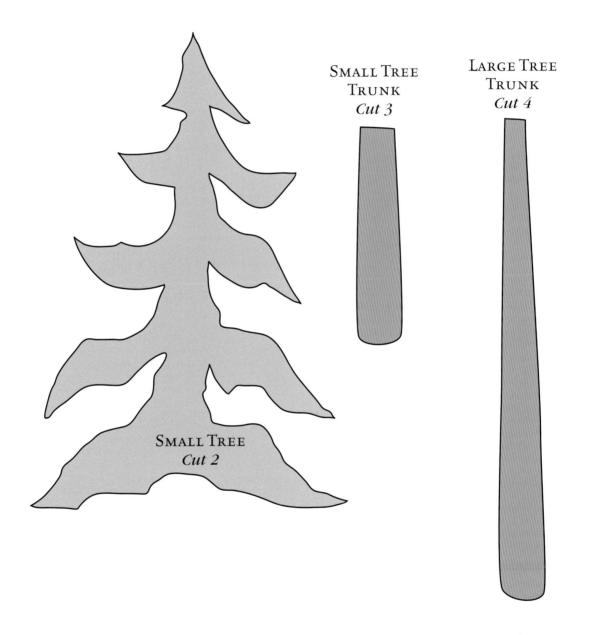

SMALL TREE
TRUNK
Cut 3

LARGE TREE
TRUNK
Cut 4

SMALL TREE
Cut 2

Tree of Life Wallhanging

Materials

Finished size is approximately 33" x 33"

Fabrics are based on 42"-wide cotton fabric that has not been washed.

1 completed Tree of Life block

Scrap of dark brown fabric for cornerstones

1/4 yard of cream fabric for sashing

1/4 yard of green print fabric for borders and binding

43" x 43" piece of batting

43" x 43" piece of backing

Cutting Instructions

• From the brown fabric, cut:
  4 squares 2-1/2" x 2-1/2" for cornerstones

• From the cream fabric, cut:
  2 strips 2-1/2" x 42"; from these strips, cut:
    4 rectangles 2-1/2" x 21-1/2" for sashing

• From the green print fabric, cut:
  4 strips 4-1/2" x 42" for borders
  5 strips 2-1/2" x 42" for binding

Assembling the Wallhanging

1. Sew a dark brown 2-1/2" x 2-1/2" square on each end of 2 cream 2-1/2" x 21-1/2" rectangles. Press toward the dark. You will have two Unit A's.

2. Sew a cream 2-1/2" x 21-1/2" rectangle on each side of the block. Press toward the block. You will have one Unit B.

3. Sew a Unit A to the top and bottom of a Unit B, as shown. Press in the direction of least amount of bulk.

4. Measure the width of the wallhanging through the center to get top and bottom border measurement. Cut two strips that length from the green print 4-1/2"-wide strips. Sew to the top and bottom. Press toward the border.

5. Measure the length of the wallhanging through the center to get side border measurement. Cut two green print strips that length from the 4-1/2"-wide strips. Sew to each side. Press toward the border.

Finishing the Wallhanging

1. Layer the backing fabric, batting, and top.

2. Hand- or machine-quilt as desired.

3. Finish the wallhanging by sewing on the binding.

General **Instructions**

Assemble the tools and supplies to complete the project. In addition to basic cutting and sewing tools, the following tools will make cutting and sewing easier: small sharp scissors to cut appliqué shapes, a rotary cutter and mat, extra rotary blades, and a transparent ruler with markings.

Replace the sewing machine needle each time you start a project, to maintain even stitches and to prevent skipped stitches and broken needles during the project. Clean the machine after every project to remove lint and to keep it running smoothly.

The projects shown are made with unwashed fabrics. If you prewash fabrics, purchase extra yardage to allow for shrinkage. The 100-percent cottons and flannels used in the wilderness quilts and accessories are from Debbie's Granola Girl® Designs collections. Ask for them by name at your local quilt shop.

Please read through the project instructions before cutting and sewing. Square the fabric before cutting and square it again after cutting 3 or 4 strips. Align the ruler accurately to diagonally cut squares into triangles. Sew with 1/4" seam allowances throughout, unless stated otherwise in the instructions, and check seam allowance accuracy to prevent compounding even slight errors. Press seams toward the darker fabric when possible. When pressing small joined pieces, press in the direction that creates less bulk.

Basic **Appliqué**

Please note that the printed appliqué templates are reversed. Tints indicate design overlap. Trace and cut the templates as printed, unless the illustrations and photos indicate to reverse the templates. For appliqués that face the opposite direction, trace and reverse the template. Trace the appliqué template to the fusible webbing with a fine tip marker or sharp pencil, allowing space to cut 1/4" beyond the traced lines. Position the fusible web on the wrong side of the appliqué fabric. Follow the web manufacturer's instructions to fuse the web to the fabric. Allow the fabric to cool, and cut along the traced line. Remove the paper backing and follow the pattern placement to position the appliqué pieces on the background fabrics.

Use lightweight tear-away stabilizer to machine appliqué. Place the stabilizer beneath the fabric layers and use a small zigzag stitch to sew around each shape, smoothly covering the raw fabric edge. If your machine has stitch options, use them to detail appliqués. After the stitching is complete, remove the stabilizer according to the manufacturer's instructions.

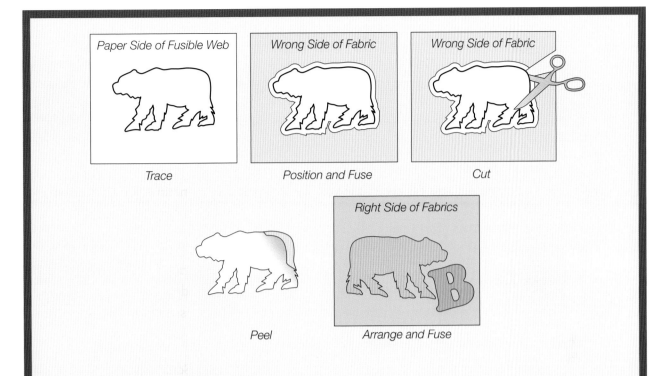

Paper Side of Fusible Web	*Wrong Side of Fabric*	*Wrong Side of Fabric*
Trace	Position and Fuse	Cut

Peel   Arrange and Fuse

Right Side of Fabrics

Basic **Binding**

Join binding strips for a continuous length. Fold the strip in half lengthwise, right sides out, and press. Match the raw edges of the folded strip to the quilt top, along a lower edge and approximately 6" from a corner, allowing approximately 6" free to join to the opposite end of the binding. Avoid placing binding seams on corners. Sew the binding to the quilt top with a 1/4" seam allowance (see Step 1).

At the first corner, stop 1/4" from the corner, backstitch, raise the presser foot and needle, and rotate the quilt 90 degrees. Fold the binding back onto itself to create a miter (see Step 2), then fold it along the adjacent seam (see Step 3), matching raw edges. Continue sewing to the next corner and repeat the mitered corner process. Where the binding ends meet, fold under one binding edge 1/4", encase the opposite binding edge, and stitch it to the quilt top.

Trim the batting and backing fabric even with the quilt top and binding. Fold the binding strip to the back of the quilt and handsew it in place with a blind stitch. Sign and date the quilt, including the recipient's name if it is a gift.

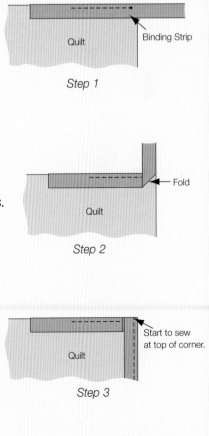

Step 1

Step 2

Step 3

About
the Author

Debbie Field, producing her work through Granola Girl® Designs has emphasized her love of the outdoors in quilts, wallhangings, books, patterns, accessories, and her own lines of fabric.

Her work is a reflection of her personal experiences since childhood with the breathtaking sights of nature and wildlife of the great northern woods.

She attributes her outdoor spirit to the warmth of her family and living an adventurous outdoor lifestyle—a tradition instilled by her parents and continued with her husband and her sons and their families.

Acknowledgements

A huge thank you to my creative team. It takes a team to produce a great book like this. Thank you to each of you for your individual talents:

Sue Longeville

Delores Farmer

Sue Carter

Amy Gutzman

Sharon Saunders

Cindy Kujawa

Visit your local quilt shop and ask for Granola Girl® Designs manufactured by Troy Corporation. Fabric collections used to make projects in this book include *Marblecake Basics, Alpine Years Ago,* and *The Great Plains.*

Choice of embroidery threads available from your favorite distributor:

Sulky® of America

www.sulky.com

1-800-874-4115